Celebrating You... Celebrating Me!
School Holidays and Life Celebrations

By Martha A. Sharts, MS.Ed.

Cover Design by Amy Rule.
Layout and design by Tonya Daugherty.

"CELEBRATING YOU... CELEBRATING ME! SCHOOL HOLIDAYS"

EAN: 978-1-59850-025-7
ISBN: 1-59850-025-2

Library of Congress Control Number
2006934789

10 9 8 7 6 5 4 3 2 1
Printed in the United States

youth light
inc.

PO Box 115 • Chapin, SC 29036
(800) 209-9774 • (803) 345-1070 • Fax (803) 345-0888
yl@youthlightbooks.com • www.youthlightbooks.com

Dedicated to

Megan and Jessica

and all the children of the world who have within themselves the capacity to make this world a better place one day at a time.

Acknowledgements

Divine inspiration comes from many sources and I believe each of us is a composite of all who have touched our lives. No one achieves without the support and encouragement of the people in his/her life. Here are some of the people in "my village."

To the building principals, with whom I have had the honor of working at Medlar View Elementary. Who have the vision and the foresight to realize that a counselor is an intricate part of the heart of a school. Who allowed me the time and the opportunity to develop a quality counseling program in line with the American School Counseling Association guidelines.

To the staff of my elementary school, who welcomed me into their classrooms to work beside them in teaching their students the "life lessons" they need to learn to be contributing citizens of our community, country and world.

To the children of my school, who like "little sponges" absorbed, learned and acquired a respect and appreciation for the diversity that is represented in our elementary school.

To the parents of my school, for their support and positive comments of how they believed their children were better prepared to go forth into the world because of their understanding and appreciation of cultures, traditions and diversity.

To Liz Dalton and Bev Reno, who for three years kept telling me I should send my lessons to a publishing house because they knew the lessons were making a difference in children's lives.

To my grandfather, Rezin Meloy, who taught me at a very early age that belief and faith in yourself was important and that you should learn to "accept who you are lumps, bumps, warts and all," because each one of us is unique.

To my parents, Omar and Bertha Meloy, who gave me roots and wings to grow and be the person I am today.

To my daughters, Megan and Jessica, who are my heart and my encouragement.

And finally, to my husband Jack, for whom I am thankful each day. Who in his quiet way has always steadfastly believed in me.

Martha A. Sharts

Table of Contents

Introduction / Overview

THE NEED FOR THIS BOOK:

School holidays provide the unique opportunity for educators to infuse character education with holiday fun. School holiday parties and activities are things that students look forward to with great anticipation. There are character education principles that can be linked with these holidays and celebrations. Many states have character education in their curriculums. In the article *Character Education in a Safe and Civil School Climate*, Charles Elbot states "there are two steps to moral behavior, knowing the right behavior, using wisdom and discrimination, then having the will and courage to skillfully do it." School holidays and life celebrations are unique opportunities to accomplish this.

HOW TO USE THIS BOOK:

This book will help you infuse culture and appreciation for diversity in your classroom. The lessons are designed to educate the students about holidays that celebrate important family and cultural events. The lessons follow the school year calendar whether you are on a traditional schedule or year round. There are ideas and materials to get your school year started. Also there are individual student materials in the chapter *Life Celebrations* which may be helpful to you in assisting children in processing the life events in which they find themselves. There are character lessons to be learned from all cultural and holiday celebrations; this book shows you how to teach those holidays and celebrations. Each lesson can be used free-standing and not at the given time of year for the holiday or can be used with just the holiday itself.

There are classroom lessons with suggested stories to share and many activities for each holiday. There is also a ParentWise newsletter that you may use as a follow-up to send home or display in your classroom or school office. Pick and choose what works best in your curriculum and adapt it to your specific needs. There may be one activity or overhead that you use with a class, or you may use all of them. There may be a lesson that you teach but without using the story to share. That is fine! Think of the lesson materials as a buffet and you are selecting the items from the buffet for your meal. As an educator I would rather have more materials to select from than less. It makes designing a lesson for a particular class much easier. And more importantly, you control the length of the lesson; design it to meet your own personal time constraints.

Only you know what works best in your educational situation. I know from experience that the greatest reward for you will be when you see the faces of children whose traditions and culture are often overlooked in the curriculum. Their eyes and expressions will mirror such gratitude that you will be glad you made the effort.

I believe that education has the capacity to change an attitude. And that an attitude can be reflected in a behavior change. As educators we are in the unique position to make this world a better place one day at a time. So let's start, *Celebrating You... And Celebrating Me!*

Martha A. Sharts

Chapter One

Back to School

In this section of the book you will find everything you need to get your students started on the track for a new school year. There is the new student interview that you can do with your students. Use the digital camera to take their picture and frame it with an Ellison die cut frame. It makes a great hall display or bulletin board. Other handouts include bookmarks, door hangers, parenting letters, and information on school safety, study skills and test taking skills.

Introducing A Brand New Student

Name _____

Grade _____ Teacher _____

I moved from

_____ .

My Favorite Food is

_____ .

One thing that makes me a good friend is

_____ .

My favorite thing to do at recess is

_____ .

My best subject in school is

_____

because

_____ .

USE THIS CHECKLIST TO PREPARE YOUR CHILDREN FOR A SAFE SCHOOL YEAR.

- Be sure your child knows his or her phone number and address, your work number, the number of another trusted adult and how to use 911 for emergencies. Make sure your child has enough change to make a phone call or carries a telephone calling card.

- Plan a walking route to school or the bus stop. Choose the most direct way with the fewest street crossings and use intersections with crossing guards. Test the route with your child. Tell him or her to stay away from parks, vacant lots, fields and other places where there are not many people around.

- Teach children-whether walking, biking, or riding the bus to school-to obey all traffic signals, signs, traffic officers and safety patrols. Remind them to be extra careful in rainy, foggy, or snowy weather.

- Make sure they walk to and from school with others such as a friend, neighbor, brother or sister. If ever stopped by a stranger while walking home, take two big steps backwards and run to the nearest house. Knock loudly on the door and ring the doorbell. Tell whoever answers what happened and to call 911.

- Teach your child never to talk to strangers or accept rides or gifts from strangers. Remember, a stranger is anyone you or your child doesn't know well or trust.

- When car pooling, drop off and pick up children as close to school as possible. Don't leave until they have entered the school yard or building.

IF YOUR CHILD IS HOME ALONE FOR A FEW HOURS AFTER SCHOOL:

- Set up rules for locking doors and windows and answering the door or telephone.

- Make sure he or she checks in with you or a neighbor immediately after school.

- Agree on rules for inviting friends over and for going to a friend's house when no adult is home.

Take time to listen carefully to children's fears and feelings about people or places that scare them or make them feel uneasy. Tell them to trust their instincts. Take complaints about bullies and other concerns seriously.

Bulletin Board Idea:

"Award Winning Study Skills!"
"Award Winning Test Taking Tips!"
or
"Award Winning Homework Tips!"

Materials:

Paper or fabric to cover the board, using the Large Ellison Die Cut patterns or pre-manufactured stars and award ribbon shapes, cut out letters for heading, tips of study skills, test taking or homework (whichever heading you are using).

Instructions:

- Cover the Bulletin Board with fabric or paper.

- Add heading in center of board.

- On award patterns (like a rosette for an award) or star patterns glue your tips that you have typed in large font on your computer.

- Place these around the heading.

Helping Your Child Be An A+ Homework Star!

1. Have your child use a planner or assignment book, so they know what is required each day.

2. Establish a regular location for homework to be done in your home. Have supplies and tools needed to complete the work available.

3. Eliminate distractions such as phone calls and television during homework time.

4. Encourage a homework schedule and have your child follow it each day to get them into a routine.

5. Introduce how to use a large planning calendar for each month and have them list long term assignments on it. Post it where they can see it in their room or on the refrigerator.

6. Each day have your child preview homework to be done and have them do the hard tasks first and the easiest last. Have your child write down the order in which he needs to do assignments, or he may number his planner.

7. Have them use a book bag to transport books and papers. Create a launching pad where your child places everything she needs to take to school the next morning.

8. Have your child keep old quizzes and tests to prepare for future tests.

9. Teach your child to review his work frequently so that he may catch mistakes early in the project.

10. Set a good example. Show your child the skills she is learning now are an important part of the things she will do as an adult. Let him see you reading books, using math, measuring for carpet and doing other things that require thought and effort.

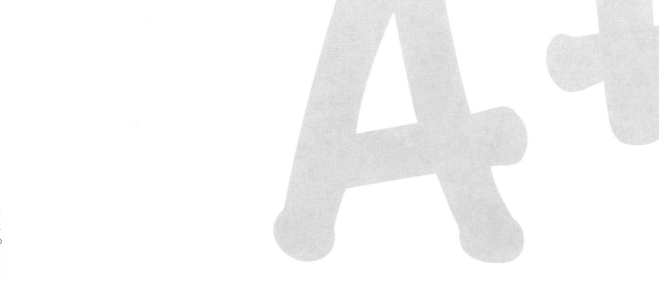

CREATING A HOMEWORK STAR

Most parents worry at one time or another how much help is too much to give their child when it comes to homework. The American Academy of Pediatrics states that children are more successful in school when parents take an active interest in homework. When parents respond in this manner children learn that what they do is important to their parents. As a first step it is always important to get to know your child's teacher. Schedule an appointment with the teacher, attend school events such as parent teacher conferences and volunteer in your child's classroom if your schedule permits. Ask the teacher about his/her homework policy, how long the assignments should take and how involved the teacher would like you to be.

Establish a regular location for homework to be done in your home. Make sure the location is well-lit and free from distractions. Eliminate phone calls, loud music and television during homework time. Have supplies and tools needed to complete homework available. Encourage your child to follow a regular schedule for study time to help him learn to get into a routine. A good rule to follow when deciding which homework needs to be done first is to do the hardest first and the easiest last. Each day encourage your child to preview the homework to be done and have him write down the order in which he needs to do assignments, or he may number his planner. You can also introduce your child to using a large planning calendar for each month and have her list long term assignments on it. Post it where she can see it in her bedroom or on the refrigerator.

Make sure your child does his own work. Your child will not learn the material if she doesn't think for herself and make her own mistakes. You can always make suggestions and help children with directions. Make sure both you and your child review the teacher's comments on completed assignments. But it is your child's job to do the work that produces the learning. Teach your child to review his work frequently so that he may catch his mistakes early in the project. Be sure to always ask about assignments, tests and quizzes. Have your child keep old quizzes and tests to prepare for future tests. Create a launching pad space in your home where your child places her book bag with completed homework inside, supplies, coat and lunch. Everything will be in one place when she needs to leave for school in the morning.

It would be nice if we could raise children who would absorb all the advice we give, but we tend to raise mirrors that reflect our own behavior. So it is important to always set a good example; show your child the skills he is learning are an important part of things he will do as an adult. Let your children see you reading books, answering emails, using math and doing other things that require thought and effort. And lastly always remember to give praise. People of all ages respond to praise. And children need encouragement and support from the people whose opinions they value most, their families. "Good job on that spelling test!" or "You've done great work on the outline for your report" can go a long way in motivating your child to complete assignments.

Be A Study Skills Star

 HAVE A HOMEWORK SCHEDULE:

4:00–4:30	Have a healthy snack, relax, listen to music or play outside.
4:30–5:30	Time to do homework! Do the hardest homework first, the easiest last!
5:30–7:00	Stop homework, do your chores, call a friend, eat dinner, play a game, play with your pet.
7:00–8:00	Finish up any remaining assignments.
8:00–9:30	Free time (if your homework is done).
9:30	Go to bed and think about how nice it is that your homework is done and how happy your teacher will be!

HAVE A HOMEWORK BOX:

Keep all supplies in a *homework box* which is kept in a safe place, like on top of the refrigerator or in the living room closet. Include scissors, sharpened pencils, markers, rulers, pens and paper (all kinds). BUT this cannot be used for anything but homework. If Mom or Dad needs scissors or paper they have to find it elsewhere. When you need to start your work everything you need is there. *NO EXCUSE TO GET OFF TRACK!*

 TOP ELEVEN HOMEWORK TIPS

1. Before you start your homework, try to clear your head of any thoughts that might distract you.

2. Do the hardest homework first, the easiest last.

3. Do your homework in a quiet place, the same location every day.

4. No speeding through your homework. Take your time. Review your work. (That means check it!)

5. Avoid developing nervous habits like playing with your hair, picking at blemishes or other things on your body. Nervous habits will distract you!

6. Always participate in class! It helps you listen and pay attention. Not to mention learn the material!

7. Take a break in the middle of your homework.

8. Use your planner to write down assignments and ask questions when you don't understand; then make notes in your planner.

9. Think for yourself in class and don't rely on asking other people for answers. This will help you learn.

10. Ask lots of questions when you don't understand.

11. Always ask for extra help if you need it. Get a tutor or a study buddy. Always have the phone number of someone in class that you can call and ask questions. Sometimes one person can explain things better than another.

Study Motivators

1. Starburst Candy

"My Students Are Homework Stars"

or

"I Am A Test Taking Star"

2. Granola Bar

"My Students Are Homework Naturals!"

or

"I Am Naturally A Great Test Taker!"

3. Fruit Rolls-ups

"Our Students Are On A Roll"

4. Smarties

"Know How to do Homework"

5. Swedish Fish

"I Am Hooked On Doing My Best"

6. Rice Krispie Treats

"Our Students Make Test Taking A Treat"

Test Taking Tips

- Get plenty of sleep the night before the test.
- Don't take the test hungry.
- Read all directions.
- Read all questions carefully
- Circle important words in the question.
- True/False look for words like never, always, all and every.
- Do the easy questions first.
- Come back to questions that stump you.
- Be sure you know what is being asked.
- Look at all choices before you answer.
- Eliminate answers you know are wrong.
- Refer to other test questions that may help you answer those you are not sure of.
- Always check your work!

ParentWise

Helping Your Child Prepare for Tests

- Instill a love of reading.
- Have your child read to you.
- Monitor child's progress in school.
- Be in frequent contact with teachers.
- Establish a regular time to study.
- Be aware of child's academic progress.
- Encourage a positive school attitude
- Don't make child nervous about tests.
- Keep home life as calm as possible before testing.

Door Hangers: Homework Schedule

Decorate and cut out these signs. Hang them on the door to your room.

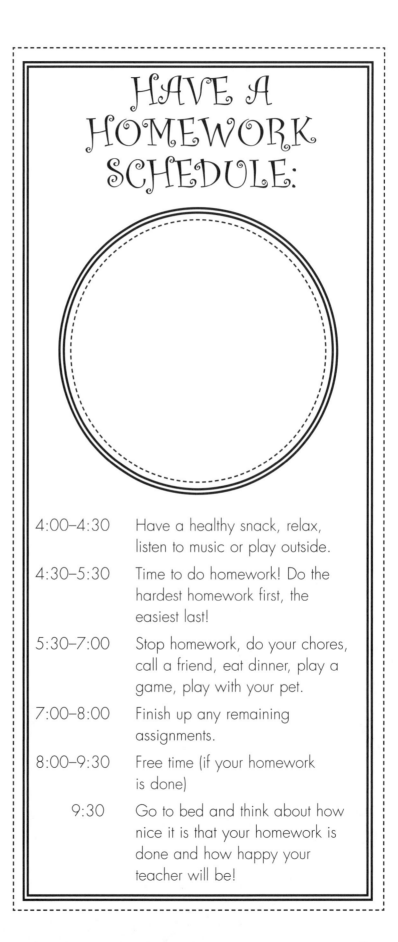

HAVE A HOMEWORK SCHEDULE:

4:00–4:30	Have a healthy snack, relax, listen to music or play outside.
4:30–5:30	Time to do homework! Do the hardest homework first, the easiest last!
5:30–7:00	Stop homework, do your chores, call a friend, eat dinner, play a game, play with your pet.
7:00–8:00	Finish up any remaining assignments.
8:00–9:30	Free time (if your homework is done)
9:30	Go to bed and think about how nice it is that your homework is done and how happy your teacher will be!

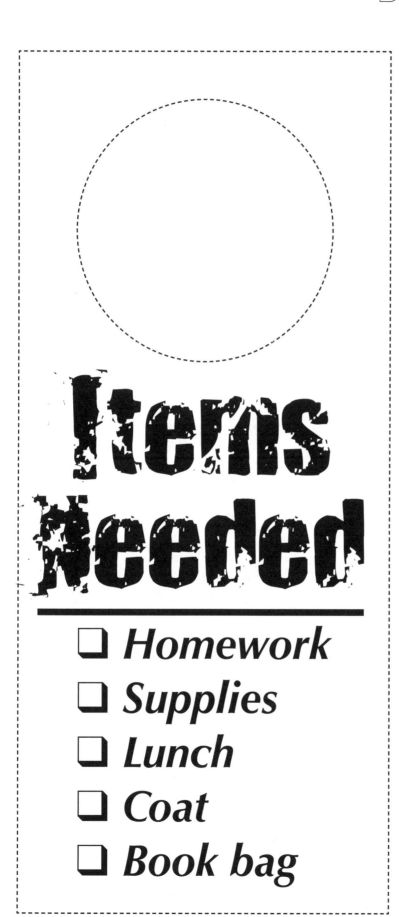

Items Needed

- ❑ *Homework*
- ❑ *Supplies*
- ❑ *Lunch*
- ❑ *Coat*
- ❑ *Book bag*

Chapter Two

Life Celebrations

There are many life celebrations that children go through that are difficult for them. Here are some processing activities that allow the student to record his/her feelings.

- My New Job Description—New baby in the home
- Movin' On—Moving to a new home and school
- Memory Book—

When a parent decides to remarry, often it is a time of adjustment for the children involved. It can raise doubts about the child's own security, cause anxiety and create confusion for the children involved. The questions and statements that follow can be easily turned into a processing activity that allows the child to put into writing some of the thoughts he would like his parent to know.

These phrases, statements and fill-in-the-blank questions can be used to create pages for a book that I affectionately call"The Wedding." After the activity is completed, call home to let the parent know the workbook is done and his/her child would like to share it with him/her.

Laminate and assemble the book. Take time to review the book with your student.

My Mom / Dad (circle one) is getting married.

This makes me feel _____. I feel _____ because _____.

My other parent knows about the wedding: ❏ yes or ❏ no.

The person my parent is marrying is called _____.

I will call this person _____. It is ❏ okay or ❏ not okay with me.

I would like _____ (the person your parent is marrying) to know _____
_____.

The wedding is going to be _____ (date) and _____ (time).

The wedding is going to be held _____.

I am going to be at the wedding: ❏ yes or ❏ no.

My part in the wedding is _____.

My parent is going on a trip called a honeymoon: ❏ yes or ❏ no.

My parent will be back from his or her honeymoon on _____ (date).

After my parent gets married, I will live with _____.

These are the people who will be living in my home _____
_____.

I will be getting stepbrothers and sisters: ❏ yes or ❏ no. Their names are _____
_____.

Draw or paste a picture of your new family here.

There will be a new pet moving in ❏ yes or ❏ no. Its name is _____.

It is a _____(type of pet).

The thing I want my parent to know I am most worried about is _____
_____.

My parent's life is changing because he or she is getting married again, and my life is changing too. I want my parent to know I still want to spend time with him or her: ❏ yes or ❏ no. And sometimes that time can be together time with all of our new family, but other times I would like it just to be the two of us.

Congratulations _____. I want you to know I love you and that will never change!

Your child,

GETTING MARRIED AGAIN

When a parent remarries it is a time of excitement, anticipation and joy for the bride and groom. But for the children it can stir up many feelings and worries about how their lives will be changing. And they wonder where are they going to fit into the new life their parent is creating? Will I be in the way? Will I still have private time with my parent? Will my parent have any time for me at all? What will I be expected to call this new person in my parent's life? Am I going to have to share a room with this new person's children? Can my stuff still be my stuff or is it now "our stuff?" Many of these anxieties can be reduced if you keep in mind some of these basic principles:

- The person you are marrying needs to have courted your child or children as much as they courted you. It is important to include children in planned events and outings so everyone can get to know each other, and your child can see this person genuinely cares about his parent and him.

- It may be hard for the child to realize that decisions that were once made by her parent now have to be shared with the new spouse. The child may resent this new pattern. Just remind her that there is a new person in the family and her opinion matters just like opinions of other family members do.

- Remember you will probably be tested in the areas of discipline. Make sure you and your future spouse have discussed and agreed upon how discipline will be handled in your new family.

- Decide on what your new spouse would like to be called. Should it be by his/her the first name or nickname? Children may have a hard time calling your new spouse Mom or Dad because they have reserved that name for a very special person, their biological mom or dad.

- Start well in advance to plan for holidays because visitation and extended family plans have to be balanced with everyone's best interests.

- Lastly, remember it is called a blended family. When you make cookies, blending the sugar and butter takes time. The process of blending two households and lives into one takes time, work, commitment and love.

My New Job Description

NEW BABY ADJUSTMENTS

When a new baby arrives in the house it can be a time of great celebration and adjustment for the family. Often children have mixed feelings of happiness and sometimes jealousy of all the attention the new baby is getting. It is an adjustment period for the child learning their "new job description" as big brother or big sister. The activity listed below can help them process the changes they are experiencing in their family and themselves. The statements and questions below can be saved on your computer and then will be ready for you to use whenever one of your students has a "new job description."

My New Job Description

By _____

My name is _____.

I have a new job description. I am a: big brother / big sister. *(Circle which you are)* You get this new job description because your mom or dad has a new baby.

I am _____ years old.

I am excited or not excited *(Circle which you are)* about my new job description.

The new baby at my house is: a boy / girl *(Circle which you have)*

The baby's name is_____.

This is the new baby. *(Draw or paste a picture of the new baby here)*

I have _____ other brothers and _____ other sisters.

So far I think being a big brother or sister for someone is O.K./not O.K. *(Circle one)*
   O. K. because _____

   Not O. K. because _____

Things I am worried about being a new big brother or sister are:
_____
_____

Things that will make me a good big brother or sister are:
_____
_____

I will tell, show or teach the new baby these 10 important things to know about how to have a good life:

1._____   6._____
2._____   7._____
3._____   8._____
4._____   9._____
5._____ 10._____
There are more important things than just 10, but that is all I have room for!

I need to improve on these things to be a better big brother / sister:

1._____

2._____

3._____

I would like my parent to know I am worried about _____

_____

This is my family (Draw or paste a picture of your family here.)

"Hi! It's Me!… Your Best Big Brother / Sister!" (Draw or paste a picture of you and your new baby sister or brother here.)

This is a list of books that you might want to read with your parent about being a new big brother/sister.

I'm A Big Brother—Joanna Cole

I'm A Big Sister— Joanna Cole

The New Baby At Your House—Joanna Cole

There's a New Baby at Our House and… I'm the Big Brother—Susan Ligon

The New Baby—Mercy Mayer

The Baby Woke Me Up. Again!—Sherry Ellis

What to Expect When The New Baby Comes Home—Hedi Murkoff

Hello Baby—Lizzy Rockwell

Big Sister Now A Story About Me And Our New Baby—Annette Sheldon

New Baby at Koko Bear's House—Vicki Lansky

Berenstain Bears and Baby Makes Five—Stan Berenstain and Jan Berenstain

Berenstain Bears' New Baby—Stan Berenstain and Jan Berenstain

Arthur's New Baby Book—Marc Brown

Arthur's Baby Book—Marc Brown

A Baby Just like Me—Susan Winter, Dorling Kindersley

Billy and The Baby—Tony Bradman

Darcy and Gran Don't Like Babies—Jane Cutler

Geraldine's Baby Brother—Holly Keller

Humphrey & Ralph—Katherine Andres

I Love My Baby Sister (Most Of The Time)—Elaine Edelman

Me Baby!—Riki Levinson

Nobody Asked Me If I Wanted a Baby Sister—Martha Alexander

ADJUSTING TO THE BABY

Depending on what position you have in the family, parent or child, the birth of a new baby can bring a multitude of different feelings. Parents can experience joy, and for the new siblings it can be a time of jealousy and feeling left out of the excitement. The new parents need to keep in mind how the other children in the family might feel, because their role in the family has changed. There are things parents can do to ease the transition.

The love and attention of parents is needed and craved by all children. When a new baby enters the family, a child's sense of security is put at risk. Because of the demands of a new baby parents must divide their attention between the children. This at times can produce feelings of jealousy, anger and illogical fear that their place in the family has been replaced. These feelings can leave, and true feelings of love and companionship can replace the once negative emotions. Even sisters and brothers who seemed at constant battle when growing up can develop into the best of friends, mentors, teachers and confidantes. Parents can work towards accomplishing this process by easing the introduction of the new sibling into the home. Try to remember your own feelings about your brothers and sisters. Here are some ideas to follow:

- Don't compare your children.

- Look at baby pictures of older children with them to put things into perspective and remind them that they were once cared for in just the same way.

- As much as possible avoid any big changes in family life like moving or changing sitters.

- Take this opportunity to discuss where babies come from-use age appropriate books.

- Look for chances where the sibling can be a participant in the care.

- Monitor gift giving; suggest that friends and family bring baby and sibling presents… or have close friends spend special time with the sibling for an outing.

- Plan special individualized time with the sibling separate from baby time, even if it is just story time or a ride in the car. Be sure to point out that this is special time set aside just for them.

- Sometimes older children regress and exhibit "babyish behaviors." Don't criticize or tell the child to "grow up." Indulge the child within reason. You may want to point out the differences between the new born and the sibling's older age.

- Don't despair if the sibling seems resentful or even disinterested. It is very hard to share attention. Brothers and sister who once fought in their homes can grow into friends. A common family history is a sturdy bond.

Movin' On

When students find out they are moving, it can be a time of uncertainty, fear and sadness but also mixed with some excitement. You can help ease this transition by making a memory book. Here are some suggestions on how to create one. Most of the activities in this booklet can be done in short pull out sessions with the student. If the student is a younger student, you may act as his or her scribe. Take digital pictures of favorite staff, classmates and teachers to place in the memory book. Often you can get information about the student's new school from the school district's website.

The statements that follow are easily saved in your computer to be printed off whenever you need them.

My Movin' On Book

FRONT COVER: MY MOVIN' ON BOOK

Use decorative fonts to add these ways to say goodbye in foreign languages:

Au Revoir

Arrivederci

Auf Wiedersehen

Adios

Goodbye

My name is _____.

I am _____years old.

I am moving from _____to_____.

Today's date is _____.

I am moving on (date) _____.

How many days left until I move? _____.

This is a picture of my school I am attending. I am going to miss you school! (Draw or paste a picture of the school here.)

The name of my school is_____.

Here is a picture of me. (Draw or paste a picture of yourself here.)

I am in grade_____.

My teachers' names are _____.

There are_____children in my class.

Some of my friends' names:_____

_____.

My home address now is_____.

My new address will be_____.

This is our home now (Draw or paste a picture here.)

What I like about my current home is:

_____.

What I don't like about my current home is:

_____.

MY FAMILY AND MY HOME (title of page)

These are the people in my family: _____

_____.

These are the people who will be moving with me:_____.

We have pets /no pets. Their names are _____

_____.

When we move: our pets will/will not come with us. We had to find a new home for them. We will give them to _____who will take really, really, good care of them.

This is a picture of my family (Draw or paste a picture of your family here.)

GOODBYE TEACHERS, GOODBYE FRIENDS, GOODBYE SCHOOL (title of new page)

At school I want to say goodbye to _____

_____.

Here is a picture of my best friends:

These are pictures of my favorite people who work at school:

Here is a picture of my class:

I will especially miss: (Write or draw here—pets, things, people, and places)

From my school: _____.

From my home: _____.

From the playground: _____.

From my school lunch: _____.

I have given my new address to my friends:

❏ Yes ❏ No (You can make cards with the addresses.)

Have my friends given me their addresses?

❏ Yes ❏ No (email, mailing addresses, phone numbers)

IMPORTANT PICTURE MEMORY PAGE

This is what I know so far about my new home:

_____.

My new school's name is : _____
(Ask your parent or guardian's help to find out.)
I will be in _____grade at my new school.
I will start my new school on (date) _____.
The language(s) used in my new school is/are:

_____.

I will go to my new school on the first day by:
❏ Bus ❏ Car ❏ Walk ❏ Bicycle
I will be taken to my new school on the first day
by:_____
Do I eat served lunch at school or do I need a
new lunch box?
Will I be eating breakfast at my new school?
Do I need to take my gym shoes?

On this page you can write or draw about the
things you are excited or worried about in your
new school:
  I am excited about:
  I am worried about:

AUTOGRAPHS/MEMORY PAGES (Class can sign and write messages here.)

LAST PAGE OF THE BOOK: Use decorative fonts
that say goodbye in these foreign languages:

Arrivederci

Auf Wiedersehen

Adios

Au revoir

Goodbye

Laminate, assemble and take time to review the
book with your student. If time permits, read the
book by Dr. Seuss The Places You Will Go

Books About Moving:

*Big Ernie's New Home: A Story for Children
Who Are Moving*—Theresa and Whitney Martin
Saying Good-bye, Saying Hello—
   Michaelene Mundy
I Like Where I Am—Jessica Harper
Just Like Home: Como En Mi Tierra—
   Elizabeth Miller
Amber Brown Is Not A Crayon—Paula Danziger
*Alexander: Who's Not: (Do you Hear Me? I
   Mean It!) Going To Move*—Judith Viorst
Boomer's Big Day—Constance McGeorge
I'm Not Moving, Mama!—
   Nancy White Carlstorm
We Just Moved—Stephen Krensky

Memory Book

There are many life transitions but none more difficult for a child than the death of a loved one. Processing the grief can be complicated because the child may not be able to discuss how he feels with his family members since they are dealing with their own grief. This Memory Book will help the child to realize that although her loved one has died, she can always hold her/him very close in her heart and in her/his mind through precious memories.

The statements that follow are easily saved on your computer and ready to be used whenever one of your students needs it. Your student will draw pictures to illustrate the statement. This will also allow him to put on paper feelings and memories and allow you the opportunity to listen and ask about the important memory she is preserving. The statements are easily personalized to recognize the holidays your student's family celebrates. Also many children have other names for the grandparents rather than grandma and grandpa. Sometimes we have nicknames for loved ones. Use those names with these statements to personalize the book even more.

Memory Book

"Ten Special Things About My _____"
at the bottom of the page add "There are lots more special things about my _____ than just one!"

When I have children of my own, I will tell them these things about _____
Then number 1- 4 with three lines to write on.

At _____ (holiday) I remember _____ (name) doing this each year!
Select the holidays your student celebrates; Passover, Diwali, Ramadan, Christmas, Chinese New Year.
Make one or two pages with the holidays your student celebrates with his/her loved one.

This is _____ (name) favorite food!
A special memory of my _____ (name) !
This was _____ (name) favorite thing to do!
_____ (name) favorite sport!
This is what I liked to play with _____ (name)!
On my birthday I remember _____ (name) doing this!

To complete the book use blue construction paper for the cover, cut three white clouds and paste on the front cover. On your computer print the following title:

My Special _____ (name of loved one)
by _____ (student's name)

Decorate the pages with stickers (stars, rainbows, smiley faces or hearts). Then laminate and assemble the book.

Be sure to call home to let your student's family know the book is complete and the student will want to share it with them. Also students often like to share their Memory Book with their classroom teacher. But more importantly take the time to look over and reflect on the completed book with your student.

Books on Grief

Michael Rosen's Sad Book—Michael Rosen

Goodbye Mousie—Robie Harris

Gentle Willow: A Story for Children About Dying—Joyce Mills

Always and Forever—Alan Durant

The Bug Cemetery—Frances Hill

The Fall of Freddie the Leaf—Leo Buscaglia

I Miss You—Pat Thomas

I Wish I could Hold Your Hand—Pat Palmer

Lifetimes: A Beautfiul Way to Explain Death to Children—Bryan Mellonie

A Story for Hippo: A Book About Loss—Simon Puttock

When Dinosaurs Die: A Guide to Understanding Death—Marc Brown

Tear Soup—Pat Schweibert, Chuck DeKlyen

CHILDREN AND GRIEF

When someone you love dies, it is a time of grief and loss for the entire family. Each person's reaction to death is individual to him/her and his/her experience. There are four main emotions that those in grief pass through: fear, anger, guilt and sadness. Children may react in these ways:

- Shock—The child may not be able to accept that the person really died and will act as if the death had not occurred.

- Physical symptoms—The child may have various complaints such as stomachaches or headaches. There may also be a concern that the child too will soon die.

- Anger—The child may be mad at the person who died because the child now feels "all alone." The child may act his/her anger out at people they are close to in the child's life because it is safe.

- Guilt—The child may feel responsible for the person's death, because the child had been angry at the person who died. Or the child may think that if the child had only been better in some way, the death would not have occurred.

- Anxiety and Fear—the child may worry about who will care for her/him and be afraid that soon another loved one will die.

- Regression—The child may revert to already outgrown behaviors.

- Sadness—The child may show a decrease in playing and other physical activity. The child may appear very quiet.

Never minimize the feeling of loss that the child has and avoid saying, "I know how you feel." Don't initiate discussion of loss if child doesn't, and when you do talk about it refrain from giving advice, being judgmental and criticizing. Realize that just because a child laughs and plays doesn't mean they didn't love or care about the person who died. Just realize that talking about it will not make it go away.

Hospice recommends the four T's in sympathy:

TALK,

TOUCH,

TEARS AND

TIME

Chapter Three

National Grandparents Day

Grandparents Day is the first Sunday after Labor Day. The idea for Grandparents Day was started by Marian Lucille Herndon McQuade. She wanted a day set aside to honor grandparents. She enlisted the help of civic, business, church and political leaders. Senator Jennings Randolph from West Virginia was especially helpful in the project. The first Grandparents Day was proclaimed in 1973 by West Virginia Governor Arch Moore. Senator Randolph introduced legislation to the Senate in 1973 to declare a special day just for grandparents. In 1978, five years after West Virginia began the tradition, the United States Congress declared the first Sunday after Labor Day as National Grandparents Day. President Jimmy Carter signed the proclamation. September was chosen as the month for this celebration to signify the "autumn years" of life.

The celebration of Grandparents Day is centered on the family. Many senior citizen groups, churches and schools honor this day with special events. Schools often host a "Grandparents Day" breakfast. Some families celebrate with a family reunion or a small private family gathering. This holiday is a perfect opportunity to teach children respect for elders. This can be encouraged by playing board games that can be enjoyed by all generations. Or have "story-telling" time, allowing grandparents to relate stories of their past, letting children know about, the "good old days." Many memories can be derived from this, and communication between many generations can be enhanced. Children can learn stories about their "roots" and patience and appreciation for the elderly. If there is a special talent a grandparent has, this could be a time to celebrate it and pass the talent on to the younger generation.

National Grandparents Day

LESSON—WHAT'S A MEMORY?

OBJECTIVES:

♟ Students will be able to explain two facts about how National Grandparents Day began.

♟ Students will be able to list three reasons why memories are important.

MATERIALS NEEDED:

Overheads, overhead projector, story, activity sheets, memory cards,"Important Stuff I Learned from my Grandparents." Follow-up interview questions, matching foreign language names for grandparents or drawing a picture activity.

OPTIONAL MATERIALS:

Recording of *Thanks for the Memories*—Rod Stewart *Thanks for the Memory ....American Song Book IV* or other artist recording of this song. Preview the lyrics because each artist starts the song differently. You may want to start the CD at a different point in the song. Bob Hope recorded it on the CDs *Thanks for the Memories* and *Thanks for the Memory*.

"STANDING OVATION APPLAUSE"

Stand up bring hands over head and clap once. Then bow from the waist. Why Standing Ovation Applause? Because our grandparents deserve our praise, and family stories and memories are things to be treasured.

1. Open the lesson with the background information on National Grandparent's Day and suggestions on how to celebrate it. Adjust the information that you share with the students depending on the age level to which you are presenting.

2. Activity- Important Stuff I Learned from my Grandparents. Have students complete it and share some of the things they have learned.

3. Reward their participation with Standing Ovation Applause.

4. Tell the students one of the things that is important about our grandparents besides the fact that they love us is they are the source of many family stories and memories. Ask the students what they think a memory is.

   OPTIONAL MATERIAL: Play a recording of the song "Thanks for the Memories" and ask the students to share what memories are talked about in this song.

5. Use the overheads in the following order to discuss memories:

   ♟ What is a memory?

   ♟ Memories are really important

   ♟ If this happens…

   ♟ Memories can be triggered

   ♟ The most important thing….

Books for Grandparents Day

6. Have students draw cards out of a cute or interesting container like fishing net and share some of their important memories.

7. End the lesson with the overhead

    🔖 The most important thing.....

And play some of the song again *Thanks for the Memories* if you have the recording.

Give teacher follow up activities.

Hooray for Grandparents Day—Nancy Carlson
The Gifts of Being Grand—Marianne Richmond
Grand-O-Grams—Marianne Richmond
Our Granny—Margaret Wild
That's What Grandparents Are For—Arlene Uslander
Halmoni's Day—Eda Coe Bercaw *
I Love Saturdays y Domingos—Alma Flor Ada *
My Nana's Remedies—Roni Capin Rivera-Ashford *
Grandfather Counts—Andrea Cheng *
Grandma U—Jeanie Franz Ransom
Just Grandma and Me—Mercer Mayer
Wilfred Gordon McDonald Partridge—Mem Fox
My Grandma Lives at the Airport—Rebecca Rudner
When Grandma Was a Girl—Bruce Lansky
Something to Remember Me By—Susan V. Bosak
Grandma was Right—Anne McKay Garris
With Love, Grandma Letter to Grandchildren—Carl B. Smith
Red, Blue and Yellow Yarn: A Tale of Forgiveness—Miriam Kosman
Grandpa's Little One—Billy Crystal
I Already Know I Love You—Billy Crystal

* Denotes Multicultural Story

What is a Memory?

It is something very important. It can help you remember what:

A rose smells like in the middle of the winter.

What turkey, dressing and mashed potatoes taste like in the middle of July.

What your mother's voice sounds like when you are on a sleep over and miss her.

How good your grandpa's hug feels when he's gone to Florida.

What your last birthday cake looked like, and it is not even close to your birthday yet!

What is a Memory?

Memories are really important. They help us remember feelings.

Positive feelings like:

Excited

Happy

Content

But sometimes memories can remind us of negative feelings like:

SAD

SCARY

DISAPPOINTED

If this happens it might help to talk to someone you trust about these memories.

WHO ARE SOME PEOPLE YOU
TRUST THAT YOU CAN TALK TO?
Counselor, teacher, parents,
grandparents, friends, etc.

---

*Sometimes when memories remind us of a
time when we made a bad choice, they can
help us from making that bad choice again!*

*Remember bad mistakes are only bad
mistakes if you keep repeating them,
memories can help you from doing that!*

Memories can be triggered by...

THINGS

like seashells, favorite rock, old ticket stubs

SMELLS

like chocolate chip cookies baking,
popcorn popping, perfume!!!!!!

SOUNDS

like music, cat purring, people's voices

TASTES

like hot chocolate, sugar cookies, fried chicken

TOUCHES

like petting a fuzzy bunny, touching a
baby's cheek or holding Grandma's hand

But the most important
thing about memory is:

it helps us keep the **people, things** and
experiences we treasure with us forever

because…

as long as we **keep these memories**
stored in our heads and our hearts
we can take them with us
wherever we go in life,

because…

they are ours **forever!**

Ideas for Classroom Activities:

- Make a memory book to share with grandparents of special memories the grandchild has of time spent with them.

- Draw a picture at the top of each calendar month reflecting a special memory the child has of his/her grandparent. Put the pages together to create a year's calendar.

- Make a thumbprint bookmark that says My Grandparent is "thumb-thing" special. Print the bookmarks on card stock. Use an ink pad of black ink and allow the thumbprint to dry completely before adding art work to it and child's name. Add ears, tail and face to make it into a cute little thumbprint creature! Then laminate.

- Make thumbprint stationery.

- Have students interview their grandparents. Share the answers with class and then display them in your class and invite the grandparents in to visit your class.

- Have your students create a list or timeline about the "important stuff" their grandparent has taught them.

- Have students locate their ancestors' homelands on a map. Place labels with students name on location.

- Have students write a poem or a story about a special memory they have of their grandparent.

- Have students make a family tree with the help of their grandparents.

ACTIVITY: MEMORY CARDS FOR LESSON
Materials needed: cards, statements, container to draw card from

1. Select memory events from the list below. Write the following statements on cards.

2. Then laminate and have a cute or interesting container like a fishing net from which to draw the cards out of.

Birthday Memory
Holiday Memory
Fun Memory
Vacation Memory
Family Memory

Grandparent Memory
Sister/Brother Memory
Mom Memory
Dad Memory

Favorite Thing Memory
Food Memory
Sound Memory
Touch Memory

IMPORTANT STUFF MY GRANDPARENT TAUGHT ME!
"My life lessons from my grandparents"
I remember I learned at age 2: _____
I remember I learned at age 4: _____
I remember I learned at age 6: _____
I remember I learned at age 8: _____
I remember I learned at age 10: _____

"Why, When I Was Your Age..."

INTERVIEWING MY SPECIAL GRANDPARENTS

DIRECTIONS:

Ask Mom or Dad when a good time would be to call your grandparent and set up a time to interview them. Then call your grandparent and set up a time for the interview. You may conduct the interview on the phone or in person, whatever works best for your family. Be sure to listen carefully to all of your grandparent's answers and ask questions. Be sure to thank your grandparent for his/her time at the end of the interview. Now let's get started!

1. Did your mom or dad have a favorite saying? What was it? Did you ever get tired of hearing it?

2. Did you have any chores to do around the house? What were they?

3. Did you have a nickname? What was it?

4. Were you ever made fun of in school? What did you do about it?

5. What was your favorite bedtime story?

6. Who was your favorite teacher? Why was he/she your favorite?

7. What subject did you like best in school?

8. Did anything important happen in history while you were in school?

9. Who was your best friend in school? What made him/her a good friend?

10. What has been the best thing that has happened to you in life? What is the worst thing that has happened?

PROCESSING THE INTERVIEW:

What was the interview like?

What was the most important thing you learned about your grandparent during the interview?

Have you had any experiences like he/she had? What were they?

Do you think you will be like the person you interviewed when you get older?

Do you think your grandparent enjoyed the interview? Why or why not?

Many Different Ways to Say Grandma

DRAW A LINE CONNECTING EACH WORD FOR
"GRANDMOTHER"
TO THE LANGUAGE IN WHICH IT IS USED:

GRANDMOTHER	LANGUAGE
1. Ya-ya	Turkish
2. Abuela	Dutch
3. Oba-chan	Spanish
4. Grand-mere	Hungarian
5. Buyuk Anne	Greek
6. Nonna	Polish
7. Grootmoeder	Italian
8. Halmoni	Japanese
9. Nagyanya	Korean
10. Babcia	French

Many Different Ways to Say Grandpa

DRAW A LINE CONNECTING EACH WORD FOR
"GRANDFATHER"
TO THE LANGUAGE IN WHICH IT IS USED:

GRANDFATHER	LANGUAGE
1. Abuelo	French
2. Seneli	Spanish
3. Avo	Dutch
4. Grand-pere	Italian
5. Dedushka	Hungarian
6. De Grootvader	Japanese
7. Halaboji	Korean
8. Nagyapa	Lithuanian
9. Oji-chan	Russian
10. Nonno	Portuguese

Answers

GRANDMOTHER PAGE 49

1. Ya-ya—Greek

2. Abuela—Spanish

3. Oba-chan—Japanese

4. Grand-mere—French

5. Buyuk Anne—Turkish

6. Nonna—Italian

7. Grootmoeder—Dutch

8. Halmoni—Korean

9. Nagyanya—Hungarian

10. Babcia—Polish

GRANDFATHER PAGE 50

1. Abuelo—Spanish

2. Seneli—Lithuanian

3. Avo—Portuguese

4. Grand-pere—French

5. Dedushka—Russian

6. De Grootvader—Dutch

7. Halaboji—Korean

8. Nagyapa—Hungarian

9. Oji-chan—Japanese

10. Nonno—Italian

Craft Idea: Portrait Cookies

SELF-PORTRAIT COOKIES OR PORTRAIT COOKIES OF GRANDPARENTS

MATERIALS NEEDED:
cookie sheet, rolling pin, prepackaged (sugar, peanut butter, chocolate) cookie dough, waxed paper, assorted candies, icing, butter knife, gingerbread man cookie cutter and plastic wrap.

1. Using the rolling pin roll out and flatten cookie dough on waxed paper.

2. Use the cookie cutter or butter knife to cut out person- shaped cookies or just use a round large glass to cut out round "faces" from the cookie dough.

3. Place the dough on a cookie sheet and bake according to manufacturer's directions.

4. Allow the cookie to cool and then complete the cookie portraits* by adding decorative icing and candy details. Make the faces by using candy coated chocolate for eyes, colored-icing hair, peppermint cheeks, and orange slices for candy ears, gumdrop noses and licorice for mouths or hair.

5. Allow icing to set and wrap with clear plastic wrap. Label each student's creation.

Portraits may be of the grandparents or the student themselves.

Bookmark

Have students make thumb print picture on bookmark to decorate it. Place thumb on black ink pad. Press down, then make thumb print on bookmark. Students may then make their thumb print into a cute thumb print creature by adding a face, ears and a tail. Have students put name and age under picture. Then laminate.

My Grandparent is "thumb-thing" special.

My Grandparent/s

(Draw or paste a picture of your grandparent or grandparents here)

GRANDPARENTS DAY

Grandparents Day is the first Sunday after Labor Day. September was chosen for this celebration to signify the "autumn years" of life. The idea was started by Marian Lucille McQuade, who wanted to honor grandparents. She enlisted the help of civic, business, church and political leaders. The first Grandparents Day was proclaimed by the governor of West Virginia in 1973. It was introduced into legislation to the Senate in 1973 by Senator Randolph. Five years after West Virginia began the tradition, the United States Congress declared the first Sunday after Labor Day as National Grandparents Day. President Jimmy Carter signed the proclamation.

The celebration of this day is centered on the family. Many senior citizen groups, religious denominations and schools honor this day with special activities. It is the perfect time for families to spend time together with their grandparents, host a family reunion or a small private family gathering. Children and families need to know their families' heritage, traditions and stories. It is part of who they are as individuals. Leo Buscaglia in his book Living, Loving and Learning wrote about the importance of children to be connected with their extended families and to know their families story. Encourage grandparents to share their stories about the "good old days," the families' "roots" or family traditions. Traditions help form the story line for a family's unique history with each generation adding or deleting traditions that enhance the family story. Grandparents Day is also a perfect time for children to learn respect, patience and appreciation for the elderly. If a grandparent has a special talent baking, woodworking or gardening, this would be a perfect time to teach the talent and pass the tradition on. Your family could take this opportunity to make a "family tree" and record your family history. These are ways to make a grandparent feel valued and respected.

*"Family faces are magic mirrors.
Looking at people who belong to us,
we see the past, the present and future."*
Gail Lumet Buckley

Scrambled Words

Name: _____ Class: _____ Date: _____

EACH LINE HAS ONE WORD THAT IS SCRAMBLED. UNSCRAMBLE THAT WORD.

1. _ _ _ _ _ _   ymeMor
2. _ _ _ _ _ _ _ _ _ _ _   aGaehtnfrdr
3. _ _ _ _ _ _ _ _ _   ritaTiond
4. _ _ _ _ _ _ _ _ _ _   aGhrnilddc
5. _ _ _ _   dKni
6. _ _ _ _ _ _ _   eRepstc
7. _ _ _ _   vLoe
8. _ _ _ _   iTem
9. _ _ _ _ _ _ _ _ _ _ _   ndraaeGnrtp
10. _ _ _ _ _ _   irnCag
11. _ _ _ _ _ _   Fmialy
12. _ _ _ _ _ _ _ _ _ _ _   aednGmorrth

SELECT YOUR ANSWERS FROM THE FOLLOWING WORDS. ANSWERS FOUND ON PAGE 59.

Caring	Tradition	Kind	Family
Memory	Grandparent	Grandmother	Time
Love	Respect	Grandfather	Grandchild

Secret Code

Name: _____ Class: _____ Date: _____

DECODE THE WORD IN EACH LINE.

1. _ _ _ _ _ _ _   txmrxbs
2. _ _ _ _ _ _   lzapvd
3. _ _ _ _ _ _ _ _ _ _   ktzwqbgpvq
4. _ _ _ _ _ _ _ _ _   stzqpspuw
5. _ _ _ _ _ _ _ _ _ _ _   ktzwqausgxt
6. _ _ _ _ _ _ _ _ _ _ _   ktzwqrztxws
7. _ _ _ _   ipwq
8. _ _ _ _   spax
9. _ _ _ _ _ _   bztpwk
10. _ _ _ _   vujx
11. _ _ _ _ _ _   axautd
12. _ _ _ _ _ _ _ _ _ _ _   ktzwqlzsgxt

SECRET CODE:

a	b	c	d	e	f	g	h	i	j	k	l	m	n	o	p	q	r	s	t	u	v	w	x	y	z
m	c	b	y	q	u	h	z	k	v	g	f	s	w	x	i	d	p	t	r	o	l	n	e	j	a

SELECT YOUR ANSWERS FROM THE FOLLOWING WORDS. ANSWERS FOUND ON PAGE 59.

Tradition	Time	Grandfather	Grandparent
Caring	Family	Love	Kind
Respect	Grandchild	Grandmother	Memory

Word Search

Name: _____ Class: _____ Date: _____

TRY TO FIND THE HIDDEN WORDS.

```
S  Z  G  R  A  N  D  P  A  R  E  N  T
C  G  R  A  N  D  F  A  T  H  E  R  R
L  A  J  H  F  D  V  J  B  Q  D  Z  A
Q  D  R  G  R  A  N  D  C  H  I  L  D
M  Y  B  I  S  E  M  D  R  G  W  T  I
E  E  E  H  N  L  S  I  J  T  M  C  T
M  I  T  R  V  G  O  P  L  M  E  B  I
O  K  D  C  K  N  G  V  E  Y  A  V  O
R  M  X  T  I  M  E  W  E  C  C  T  N
Y  I  M  J  N  K  Y  K  J  A  T  D  W
G  R  A  N  D  M  O  T  H  E  R  Y  F
S  E  I  N  H  T  X  G  Y  S  F  J  D
A  R  S  R  E  R  Y  M  M  I  T  K  F
```

SELECT FROM THE FOLLOWING WORDS. ANSWERS FOUND ON PAGE 59.

Grandfather	Grandmother	Love	Time
Grandparent	Memory	Respect	Grandchild
Tradition	Caring	Family	Kind

Answers

Scrambled Words page 56

1. Memory
2. Grandfather
3. Tradition
4. Grandchild
5. Kind
6. Respect
7. Love
8. Time
9. Grandparent
10. Caring
11. Family
12. Grandmother

Secret Code page 57

1. Respect
2. Family
3. Grandchild
4. Tradition
5. Grandmother
6. Grandparent
7. Kind
8. Time
9. Caring
10. Love
11. Memory
12. Grandfather

Word Search page 58

```
•   •   G   R   A   N   D   P   A   R   E   N   T
C   G   R   A   N   D   F   A   T   H   E   R   R
•   A   •   •   F   •   •   •   •   •   •   •   A
•   •   R   G   R   A   N   D   C   H   I   L   D
M   •   •   I   •   E   M   •   •   •   •   •   I
E   •   •   •   N   L   S   I   •   •   •   •   T
M   •   •   •   •   G   O   P   L   •   •   •   I
O   •   •   •   K   •   •   V   E   Y   •   •   O
R   •   •   T   I   M   E   •   E   C   •   •   N
Y   •   •   •   N   •   •   •   •   •   T   •   •
G   R   A   N   D   M   O   T   H   E   R   •   •
•   •   •   •   •   •   •   •   •   •   •   •   •
•   •   •   •   •   •   •   •   •   •   •   •   •
```

Chapter Four

Halloween

Many school districts do not allow classroom celebrations of Halloween because of the connections to Satan, ghosts and witchcraft. But for those schools that do allow the celebration of the holiday, here is the history of the holiday and some suggestions for classroom activities and bulletin boards.

HISTORY OF HALLOWEEN

Halloween can trace its origin back to the ancient Celtic festival of Samhain pronounced sow-in. The Celts lived 2,000 years ago in an area of the world that is known as the United Kingdom, northern France and Ireland. The people who lived in this area celebrated their new year on November 1. To them this day signified the end of summer and the harvest and the beginning of the cold, dark winter. The winter was a season of the year the Celts often associated with death. On the night of October 31, they celebrated Samhain. During this night, they believed the ghosts of the dead returned to earth often damaging crops and causing trouble. The Celtic people believed that the presence of other spirits made it easier for the priests to make predictions about the future.

To honor the event, the people built huge bonfires where they burned crops and animals as sacrifices to honor Celtic deities. During the celebration, the Celts wore costumes and tried to tell each other's fortunes. When the celebration was over, they re-lit their hearth fires, which they had extinguished earlier in the day, with fire from the sacred bonfire. This they believed would help protect them during the coming winter.

The Romans by 43 A.D. had conquered the majority of the Celtic region. In the four hundred year reign that followed, the Romans combined two of their own festivals with the Celtic festival of Samhain. The first festival they combined was the Roman festival of Feralia, a day in late October when Romans traditionally commemorated the passing of the dead. The second festival was a day to honor Pomona, the Roman Goddess of fruit and trees. The symbol of Pomona and its incorporation into the celebration of Samhain probably explains the tradition of "bobbing" for apples practiced today on Halloween.

By the 800's Christianity had spread into the Celtic regions. By the seventh century Pope Boniface designated November 1 All Saints Day, a time to honor saints and martyrs. It is thought that this was an attempt to replace the Celtic festival of Samhain. November 1 was also referred to as All-hallows or All-hallowmas (Middle English Alholowmesse meaning All Saints' Day). Therefore the night before which was Samhain began to be called All-hallows Eve and eventually Halloween.

As people moved to American from Europe, they brought with them their Halloween customs. In New England in the early history of our country Halloween celebrating was severely limited because of a strict Protestant belief system. It was much more common to celebrate Halloween in Maryland and the southern states. By the middle of the nineteenth century annual celebrations were common, but Halloween was not yet celebrated everywhere in the country. With the second wave of immigrants to America in the nineteenth century, more people brought Halloween traditions. Many of these immigrants were Irish fleeing the potato famine of 1846.

Taking the Irish and English traditions, people in America began dressing up in costumes and going from house to house asking for food or money. This became the "trick-or-treat" tradition we know today. The American tradition of "trick

Great Pumpkin Facts

or treating" probably can be traced back to the All Souls' Day parades in England. During this festival, underprivileged citizens would beg for food and would receive "soul cakes" in return for their promise to pray for the person's dead relatives. The church at the time actually endorsed this practice because it replaced the practice of children going from door to door in the neighborhood and being given ale, food and money.

The tradition of dressing in costumes has European and Celtic roots. A very long time ago when winter was a time of scarce food supplies and days were short many people worried and were afraid of the dark. They believed that on Halloween ghosts came back to Earth and that people would bump into them if they left their homes. To avoid being recognized by these spirits, people would wear masks. It was hoped that the person wearing the mask would be mistaken for another spirit. To keep the spirits away from their houses the people would place bowls of food outside to satisfy them and keep them from entering their homes.

Halloween was more about community and neighborhood gatherings in the 1800's than about ghosts, pranks and witchcraft. In the 1920's and 1930's the holiday became community centered with parades and area wide parties. Between 1920 and 1950 the centuries old practice of trick or treating was revived. This was a way for the entire community to celebrate without spending a great deal of money. This new American tradition has continued to grow into a large commercial holiday.

GREAT PUMPKIN FACTS

- Pumpkins are fruits not vegetables. A pumpkin is a type of squash and a member of the gourd family. Melons, cucumbers and gherkins (taste like cucumbers but no bitterness!) are all in the same family.

- Pumpkins have been grown in North America for five thousand years. They are native ("native" means they have always grown here) to the western hemisphere.

- In 1584, after French explorer Jacques Cartier explored the St. Lawrence region of North America, he reported finding "great melons" which were pumpkins! The name was translated into English as pompions which has developed into the modern word "pumpkin."

- Pumpkins are good for you! They are both low in sodium, fat and calories but high in good things like Vitamin A, Vitamin B, potassium and iron.

- You can save last year's pumpkin seeds to grow new pumpkins next year. Plant the seeds in late June. They take about 90-120 days to grow. Pick the pumpkins in late October when they are bright orange.

- Pumpkins are 90% water.

- Pumpkin flowers are edible

- In colonial times, Native Americans roasted long strips of pumpkin in an open fire. They also flattened and dried them, then used them for mats.

ACTIVITY: Guess how many pumpkin seeds you will find in a pumpkin, then cut the top off and count how many there actually are!

The Story of "Stingy Jack"

OR OTHERWISE KNOWN
AS A JACK-O-LANTERN

Carving pumpkins has long been a Halloween tradition. It has its roots in an Irish myth about a gentleman named "Stingy Jack." "Stingy Jack" invited the Devil to have a drink with him. Jack did not want to have to pay for the drink. So he convinced the Devil to turn himself into a coin so Jack could pay for their drinks. After the Devil obliged Jack, he decided to keep the coin so he placed it in his pocket next to a silver cross. The cross prevented the Devil from turning back into himself. After a while Jack freed the Devil under the condition he not bother him for one year. And if Jack should die the Devil would not claim his soul. The next year Jack tricked the Devil into climbing a tree to pick some fruit. While the Devil was up in the tree Jack carved a cross into the tree's bark. So the Devil was stuck up in the tree until he promised not to bother Jack for ten more years. Soon after this Jack died and God did not want such a tricky person in heaven and the Devil kept his word and didn't allow his soul into hell. So Jack went off into the dark of night with only a small piece of burning coal to light his path. Jack put the coal into a carved out turnip and has been wandering the earth with it ever since. The Irish began to call this ghostly shape "Jack of the Lantern" then simply "Jack O' Lantern." In Scotland and Ireland folks began carving scary faces into potatoes or turnips and put them in their windows to scare off "Stingy Jack." In England they carve beets. When people from these countries came to America they soon found that our native pumpkins made the perfect Jack O'Lantern.

Halloween

LESSON—STRANGER DANGER

OBJECTIVES:

- ❧ Students will be able to tell three facts about the history and traditions of Halloween.

- ❧ Students will be able to list four Halloween Trick or Treating Safety Tips.

- ❧ Students will be able to list four behaviors that when practiced can keep you safe from strangers.

MATERIALS NEEDED:

Items for Hot Goblin Game, Halloween Safety Tips for Trick or Treating (one for each student), Halloween song lyrics either on overhead or one for each student, overheads, overhead projector, story to share and follow up activities for teacher.

OPTIONAL MATERIAL:

Halloween Music CD appropriate for children. You could open your lesson with the song Ex. Monster Mash or Ghost Busters.

"BAT APPLAUSE"

Hold hands in front with your fingers extended. Link thumbs. flap extended fingers like bat wings. Fly your bat, flapping the wings across the front of you four times. Why Bat Applause? It is Halloween and you are a flying bat!

1. Open lesson with background information on Halloween and some of the traditions and how they evolved. Or use Great Pumpkin Facts. Adjust the information you give to be appropriate to the age of the students you are teaching. You could start the lesson by asking the children, "What is the most fun thing about Halloween?" Or what their costume is going to be, or what is the best Halloween custom or tradition?

   • Use Halloween CD to open lesson if you have one available.

2. Pass out song sheets and sing a Halloween song.

3. Pass out Halloween Safety Tips for Trick or Treating.

4. Point out to the children that many of these Safety Tips have to do with protecting you from strangers.

5. Use overheads in this order to discuss Stranger Danger. Tell them all the people in the world fall into three different categories; people you know, people you don't know and people you don't know but who are probably okay.

   - ❧ Stranger Danger
   - ❧ Why is this
   - ❧ More Tips
   - ❧ Never, Never, Never
   - ❧ Let's Practice: Use "Bat Applause" to reward participation

Books on Halloween

6. Play Hot Goblin Game

7. Read a Halloween Story

8. Overhead

   * Strangers and Dangers—
     Review and wrap up lesson.

9. Tell everyone to have a safe and Happy Halloween.

BOOKS FOR HALLOWEEN

Big Pumpkin—Erica Silverman

The Little Old Lady Who Was Not Afraid of Anything—Linda Williams

Cinderella Skeleton—Robert D. San Souci

Trick or Treat Smell My Feet—Diane de Groat

Runaway Pumpkin—Kevin Lewis

Clifford's First Halloween—Norman Bridwell

Clifford and the Halloween Parade—Norman Bridwell

Franklin's Halloween—Paulette Bourgeois

Arthur's Halloween Costume—Lillian Hoban

Arthur's Halloween—Marc Brown

Harriet's Halloween Candy—Nancy Carlson

The Hallo-wiener—Dav Pilkey

The Biggest Pumpkin Ever—Steven Kroll

Miss Fiona's Stupendous Pumpkin Pies—Mark Kimball Moulton

Stranger Danger

PEOPLE YOU MEET CAN BE
DIVIDED INTO THREE CATEGORIES:
- *People I know*
- *People I don't know*
- *People I don't know who are okay*

WHO ARE *People I know* ?

Neighbors, Friends, Friend's Parents, Relatives, Teachers, Parent's Friends

DID WE LEAVE ANYBODY OUT?

Stranger Danger

WHO ARE *People I don't know* ?

That's an easy one they are anyone you don't know. It doesn't matter if they are nice looking, friendly, you've seen them around the neighborhood or they talked to you once.

WHO ARE *People I don't know who are probably okay* ?

Police   Firefighters   Security Officers
Doctors   Nurses

A mother with children

Store salesperson with a name tag on

A person at an information booth at the mall or another public place.

Because not everyone in the world is a nice person.

If you are in a public place
like a mall, store or amusement park
and get separated from your parents,
go to the checkout counter, or to a
security office and quickly tell the
person in charge that you have
lost your parents, and need help!

Do not get into a car or go anywhere
with a person unless your parents
have told you it is okay.

More Tips to be Safe:

If someone follows you in a car when you are walking outside, *stay away* from them!

Don't go near the car or inside it.

Get to a *crowded, well-lit place*. Or to the nearest *neighbor's house* you know, where others can help.

If someone tries to take you away quickly, yell really loud:

"This person is trying to take me away!"

"This is not my mother or father!"

PRACTICE TIME:

Yell in your loudest voice!

Try to make the noise come from deep inside you—like from your stomach.

Always use the buddy system, go places with friends and never alone.

NEVER, NEVER, NEVER

Respond to anyone you don't know well to give directions or look for a lost pet or who tells you your parent is in trouble and they will take you to them.

Always ASK PERMISSION BEFORE YOU GO SOMEWHERE. Always TELL AN ADULT WHERE YOU ARE GOING.

If someone you don't know well wants to take your picture,

say NO!

(Unless it is a school photographer! Or you are getting your pictures taken for a special occasion.)

Let's Practice What to Do...

You are walking home from school when a person pulls up alongside of you and asks directions.

What do you do?

You are at the most wonderful amusement park with your family. You are watching this really cool roller coaster in which you flip upside down. You look up and your family is gone.

What do you do?

Someone has been hanging around the basketball courts watching you and your friends play. The guy looks all right. He shows up one day when you are walking home and offers you a ride. He won't take no for an answer and keeps following you with his car.

What do you do?

Your friends and you are playing. He gets bored and wants you to go down to the river to play.

What do you do?

Someone stops you at the park and wants to take your picture.

What do you do?

A stranger is a person whom you have never met. You may have seen this person before but don't know anything about this person. Strangers don't look like crooks on TV, aliens from space or monsters. They look like regular ordinary people.

The BIG DEAL is that some people are not good people. You can't tell by looking at them.

HERE IS WHAT TO DO:

1. Be aware of dangerous situations
2. Trust your feelings of not being comfortable or scared and get away.
3. Know what to do. Think, Say No, Shout, Tell, Run and go to the nearest safe place.
4. Stick together—Safety in numbers
5. Ask Parents First—Before going anywhere

Halloween Safety Tips for Trick or Treating

Walk, slink and tiptoe on sidewalks, not in the street or across yards and flowerbeds.

Look both ways when crossing the street to check for low flying bats and goblins.

Cross the street only at the corners and where there are crosswalks. Carry a flashlight. Don't cross the street between parked cars and trucks.

Make sure your costume is made of a type of fabric that reflects light. Or you can put reflective tape on your costume and your laser sword, broom and any ghosts you take with you.

Take an adult or responsible youth with you.

Visit homes which have a porch light on and only in areas with which you are familiar. Plan your route with your family.

Only accept treats at the door, and never, never go inside a stranger's house.

Be cautious of any animals and people you don't know.

Have a grownup inspect your treats before you eat them. And when in doubt, throw it out!

Keep away from candles and open fires.

Halloween Songs

TWELVE DAYS OF HALLOWEEN
Sung to the tune of "The Twelve Days of Christmas"

On the **first day** of Halloween, my mother gave to me, **a Trick or Treat bag full of candy.**

On the **second day** of Halloween my mother gave to me, **two bats flying** and a Trick or Treat bag full of candy.

On the **third day** of Halloween my mother gave to me, **three pieces of candy corn**, two bats flying and a Trick or Treat bag full of candy.

On the **fourth day** of Halloween my mother gave to me **four friendly ghosts**, three pieces of candy corn, two bats flying and a Trick or Treat bag full of candy.

On the **fifth day** of Halloween my mother gave to me **five Jack-O-Lanterns**, four friendly ghosts, three pieces of candy corn, two bats flying and a Trick or Treat bag full of candy.

On the **sixth day** of Halloween my mother gave to me **six popcorn balls**, five Jack-O-Lanterns, four friendly ghosts, three pieces of candy corn, two bats flying and a Trick or Treat bag full of candy.

On the **seventh day** of Halloween my mother gave to me **seven apples for bobbing**, six popcorn balls, five Jack-O-Lanterns, four friendly ghosts, three pieces of candy corn, two bats flying and a Trick or Treat bag full of candy.

On the **eighth day** of Halloween my mother gave to me **eight super hero costumes**, seven apples for bobbing, six popcorn balls, five Jack-O-Lanterns, four friendly ghosts, three pieces of candy corn, two bats flying and a Trick or Treat bag full of candy.

On the **ninth day** of Halloween my mother gave to me **nine caramel apples**, eight super hero costumes, seven apples for bobbing, six popcorn balls, five Jack-O-Lanterns, four friendly ghosts, three pieces of candy corn, two bats flying and a Trick or Treat bag full of candy.

On the **tenth day** of Halloween my mother gave to me **ten black cats**, nine caramel apples, eight super hero costumes, seven apples for bobbing, six popcorn balls, five Jack-O-Lanterns, four friendly ghosts, three pieces of candy corn, two bats flying and a Trick or Treat bag full of candy.

On the **eleventh day** of Halloween my mother gave to me **eleven chocolate bars**, ten black cats, nine caramel apples, eight super hero costumes, seven apples for bobbing, six popcorn balls, five Jack-O-Lanterns, four friendly ghosts, three pieces of candy corn, two bats flying and a Trick or Treat bag full of candy.

On the **twelfth day** of Halloween my mother gave to me **twelve pieces of bubble gum**, eleven chocolate candy bars, ten black cats, nine caramel apples, eight super hero costumes, seven apples for bobbing, six popcorn balls, five Jack-O-Lanterns, four friendly ghosts, three pieces of candy corn, two bats flying and a Trick or Treat bag full of candy.

HALLOWEEN IS HERE
Sung to the tune of Row, Row, Row Your Boat

Halloween, Halloween, Halloween is here
Halloween is lots of fun, Halloween is here.

Try dividing the class into groups and singing this song in rounds.

Halloween Craft & Bulletin Board

STRING JACK-O-LANTERNS

MATERIALS NEEDED:

Orange string or yarn, small balloons, glue, water, disposable containers to hold glue/water mixture, newspaper, waxed paper, tape, black construction paper and needle.

- ❦ Cover tables or desks with newspaper

- ❦ Add a little water to thin out glue

- ❦ Have students blow up balloon to the size of a small pumpkin.

- ❦ Distribute yarn or string about 6 yards per student.

- ❦ Have students dip string/yarn into glue mixture then squeeze out excess between fingers.

- ❦ Students then wrap string around the balloon in a diagonal pattern. Then wrap in a random pattern leaving some open space, because it adds interest.

- ❦ Place on wax paper to dry. Tie a piece of string to use for hanging.

- ❦ Place a piece of tape with students name on string.

- ❦ After the string has dried, using construction paper have students tear out eyes, nose and a mouth design and glue on pumpkin.

- ❦ Teacher uses a needle to pop the balloon if it hasn't popped already.

- ❦ Hang Jack-O-Lanterns and enjoy!

BULLETIN BOARD IDEA

Make a totem pole out of different shapes of jack-o-lantern cutouts. Have three friendly bats flying around the totem pole of jack-o-lanterns. Message on bulletin board:

Through Cooperation We Accomplish More!

HALLOWEEN SAFETY

Most children love Halloween, they like to get dressed up in a costume and get free candy. There are many ways to keep your child safe at Halloween. But the excitement of the season can sometimes make them forget to be careful. Using common sense on your part can do much to stop any accident from happening. Here are some tips to consider:

- Help select or make a costume that will be safe for your child. Make it fireproof; and if there is a mask, make sure the holes are large enough so your child can have good peripheral vision. Consider using face paint instead of a mask. Use reflective tape on the costume so your little ghost will be seen after dark. Reflective tape can be found in hardware, bicycle or sporting goods stores.

- If you use candles in your jack-o-lanterns make sure they are far enough out of the way that your little trick or treaters won't accidentally knock them over or be set on fire.

- If your child is carrying a prop like a laser sword, broom or pitch fork make sure the tips are smooth and flexible enough not to allow an injury if your little goblin falls on them.

- No child should be allowed to go trick-or-treating alone. Always have an adult or a responsible older youth accompany them.

- Tell children to turn down all invitations to enter homes. No exceptions!

- Make sure goody bags are light in color and easily seen. You can use reflective tape to decorate them.

- Remind children to cross the street only at cross walks and at the corner. Do not dart out from between parked cars.

- Map out the trick-or-treat route with your child.

- Visit only those houses with the lights on.

- Walk, do not run. Walk on sidewalks and driveways, not across yards and flower beds.

- Carry a flashlight or a glow stick.

- Check your children's candy before they eat it. When in doubt about a piece of candy or homemade treat, throw it out!

- Teach your children to say thank you at each home they visit for their treat.

- Pin a slip of paper with your child's name, address and phone number on it, inside their costume in case they get separated from the group.

- Serve your children a filling meal or trick or treat snack before they leave. They will be less likely to sneak a piece of candy that you haven't checked yet.

Making Halloween a fun, safe and happy time for your family will build memories that will last a lifetime. The traditions you taught them will carry on to their own families someday!

Scrambled Words

Name: _____ Class: _____ Date: _____

EACH LINE HAS ONE WORD THAT IS SCRAMBLED. UNSCRAMBLE THAT WORD.

1. selppA   _ _ _ _ _ _
2. pPcrnoo   _ _ _ _ _ _ _
3. rdnFsei   _ _ _ _ _ _ _
4. yCand   _ _ _ _ _
5. arTte   _ _ _ _ _
6. pknuimPs   _ _ _ _ _ _ _ _
7. nuF   _ _ _
8. mCouset   _ _ _ _ _ _ _
9. iFlmya   _ _ _ _ _ _
10. grSaetrn   _ _ _ _ _ _ _ _
11. ikTrc   _ _ _ _ _
12. Syatef   _ _ _ _ _ _
13. oneaHllwe   _ _ _ _ _ _ _ _ _
14. atBs   _ _ _ _
15. saCt   _ _ _ _

SELECT YOUR ANSWERS FROM THE FOLLOWING WORDS.
THE ANSWERS ARE FOUND ON PAGE 79.

Stranger	Popcorn	Candy	Apples	Family
Bats	Halloween	Costume	Pumpkins	Cats
Treat	Fun	Safety	Friends	Trick

Name: _____ Class: _____ Date: _____

TRY TO FIND THE HIDDEN WORDS.

```
C  Z  F  R  I  E  N  D  S  J  S  G  U
O  N  Q  H  W  S  V  W  A  M  O  W  K
S  S  P  V  A  U  A  N  K  D  U  I  F
T  T  Z  U  C  L  C  F  A  M  I  L  Y
U  R  W  P  M  A  L  A  E  Q  F  T  N
M  A  W  U  O  P  C  O  T  T  O  W  R
E  N  B  F  A  P  K  A  W  S  Y  U  B
X  G  Z  U  T  L  C  I  N  E  V  W  A
T  E  D  N  R  E  P  O  N  D  E  D  A
S  R  B  N  E  S  F  P  R  S  Y  N  Q
I  S  I  A  A  A  L  I  A  N  B  Q  I
E  X  S  C  T  C  P  F  H  R  C  W  Y
Z  E  I  Y  K  S  F  B  P  R  F  P  E
```

SELECT FROM THE FOLLOWING WORDS. THE ANSWERS ARE FOUND ON PAGE 79.

Halloween	Apples	Popcorn	Friends	Family
Bats	Treat	Costume	Safety	Fun
Candy	Trick	Stranger	Pumpkins	Cats

Secret Code

Name: _____ Class: _____ Date: _____

DECODE THE WORD IN EACH LINE.

1. bcyjaxdy _ _ _ _ _ _ _ _
2. vievukab _ _ _ _ _ _ _ _
3. pjafn _ _ _ _ _
4. tjoomldda _ _ _ _ _ _ _ _ _
5. rjcb _ _ _ _
6. gykdafb _ _ _ _ _ _ _
7. pjcb _ _ _ _
8. vmvpmya _ _ _ _ _ _ _
9. gjekon _ _ _ _ _ _
10. cydjc _ _ _ _ _
11. bjgdcn _ _ _ _ _ _
12. gia _ _ _
13. pmbcied _ _ _ _ _ _ _
14. jvvodb _ _ _ _ _ _
15. cykpu _ _ _ _ _

SECRET CODE:

a	b	c	d	e	f	g	h	i	j	k	l	m	n	o	p	q	r	s	t	u	v	w	x	y	z
n	s	t	e	m	d	f	v	u	a	i	w	o	y	l	c	q	b	x	h	k	p	j	g	r	z

SELECT YOUR ANSWERS FROM THE FOLLOWING WORDS.
THE ANSWERS ARE FOUND ON PAGE 79.

Costume	Halloween	Candy	Popcorn	Fun
Trick	Safety	Bats	Cats	Apples
Stranger	Friends	Family	Pumpkins	Treat

Scrambled Words page 76

1. Apples
2. Popcorn
3. Friends
4. Candy
5. Treat
6. Pumpkins
7. Fun
8. Costume
9. Family
10. Stranger
11. Trick
12. Safety
13. Halloween
14. Bats
15. Cats

Secret Code page 78

1. Stranger
2. Pumpkins
3. Candy
4. Halloween
5. Bats
6. Friends
7. Cats
8. Popcorn
9. Family
10. Treat
11. Safety
12. Fun
13. Costume
14. Apples
15. Trick

Word Search page 77

```
C  •  F  R  I  E  N  D  S  •  •  •  •
O  •  •  H  •  S  •  •  •  •  •  •  •
S  S  P  •  A  •  A  •  •  •  •  •  •
T  T  •  U  •  L  C  F  A  M  I  L  Y
U  R  •  P  M  A  L  A  E  •  •  •  •
M  A  •  •  O  P  C  O  T  T  •  •  •
E  N  •  F  •  P  K  A  W  S  Y  •  •
•  G  •  U  T  L  C  I  N  E  •  •
T  E  •  N  R  E  •  O  N  D  E  •  •
•  R  B  •  E  S  •  •  R  S  Y  N  •
•  •  I  A  A  •  •  •  •  N  •  •  •
•  •  •  C  T  •  •  •  •  •  •  •  •
•  •  •  •  K  S  •  •  •  •  •  •  •
```

Chapter Five

National Family Day

What is a family?

WHAT IS FAMILY DAY?

It is a day that has become a national effort for parental involvement as a way to reduce substance abuse in children and teens. Family Day stresses the importance of regular family activities to promote parent-child communication. It also encourages regular family dinners as a way to promote this. The National Center of Addiction and Substance Abuse at Columbia University (CASA) launched Family Day – A Day to Eat Dinner with Your Children™ as a yearly event to take place on the fourth Monday of each September.

Since 1996 CASA research has consistently shown that the more children eat dinner with their families, the less likely they are to abuse drugs, smoke or drink alcohol. CASA research consistently shows that frequent family dinners make a difference in teens' lives. Compared to teens who have five to seven family dinners in a typical week, teens who dine with their families fewer than three nights in a typical week are two times likelier to have tried marijuana, more than twice as likely to have tried cigarettes and one and a half times likelier to have tried alcohol, according to CASA's The Importance of Family Dinners III. The report also found that frequent family dinners are also associated with higher academic performance. Teens who have dinner with their families five to seven times in a typical week are likelier to get mostly A's and B's in school compared to teens who dine with their families fewer than three times per week. Academic performance is associated with substance abuse risk; Teens who report receiving grades of C or lower are at twice the risk of substance abuse as those who report receiving all A's or A's and B's.

FAMILY DAY PROCLAMATIONS AND SUPPORT

Since 2001 the President and the governors of numerous states and the mayors and executives of hundreds of cities and counties have issued Family Day – A Day to Eat Dinner with Your Children™ proclamations. Family Day has also received support each year from national corporate sponsors these are listed on their website.

National Family Day

LESSON—WHAT IS A FAMILY?

OBJECTIVES:
- At the end of the lesson the students will be able to describe three functions of a family.

- At the end of the lesson the students will be able to explain two ways families are alike and two ways they are different.

- At the end of the lesson the students will be able to explain why it is important to spend time with your family.

MATERIALS NEEDED:
A story for the lesson that you have selected. "Pass It On" game materials, overheads, overhead projector and activity sheets.

OPTIONAL MATERIAL:
Recording of the song "We Are Family" music and lyrics by Bernard Edwards, Nile Rogers

APPLAUSE: —"CELEBRATE MY FAMILY"
Use the rhythm to the song"Celebrate:"
Clap your hands once in front of you, raise one hand in the air and say "Celebrate my family, Come On!" Use this when students participate to help keep their attention and reward them.

1. Open the lesson by talking about the background of National Family Day and why it is important.

   - If you have the recording "We Are Family," open the lesson with that; then transition into talking about the background of National Family Day.

2. Ask students what definition they would give for the word "family." How would they describe what is a family?

3. Use the overheads in this order to discuss the concept of family.

   - What is a family?

   - A family is…
   Use the worksheet after this overhead: *Words that describe my family*. Follow up discussion by asking students to share some of their describing words and why they feel that way. Then continue to next overhead.

   - There are lots of different names for families.
   After this overhead is discussed, do the game activity of *"Simon Says."* Introduce the game and do the follow-up questions listed with the game.

4. Read a story you have selected about a family from the list. Do follow-up questions for discussion relating to the lesson theme.

5. Play the game "Pass It On."

6. End the lesson with the transparency "A family is…"

7. Leave the drawing activity "Introducing My Family" with the classroom teacher as a follow-up

Books About Family

The Worm Family—Tony Johnson

Our Tree Named STEVE—Alan Zweibel

The Relatives Came—Cynthia Rylant

How My Parents Learned to Eat—Ina R. Friedman*

All Kinds of Families—Norma Simon*

The Family Book—Todd Parr*

Families—Susan Kuklin (This is a composite of interviews with lots of different types of families.) *

Families Are Forever—Craig Shemin (adoption theme)

Families are Different—Nina Pellegrini *

Who's In a Family?—Robert Skutch *

All Families Are Different—Sol Gordon, Ph.D. *

Rosie's Family An Adoption Story—Lori Rosove

A Mother for Choco—Keilko Kasza (adoption theme)

The Graves Family Goes Camping—Patricia Polacco

Families—Ann Morris *

All Families Are Special—Norma Simon*

Me And My Family Tree—Joan Sweeney

Clifford's Family—Norman Bridwell

* Diversity Themes

What is a family?

It is a group of people who may or may
not be *related* to you. Sometimes you have
the *same last name*, sometimes you don't.

These people may be *old* or they may be *young*.
These people may be *rich*, *poor* or some place *in between*.
These people may be many different *colors*.
These people may be *short* or *tall*, *fat* or *skinny*,
hairy or *bald*, *funny* or *serious*, *plain* or *fancy*.

These people sometimes *live with you*,
and sometimes they don't and you visit them.

Some of these people may not be people at all...
but *pets*!

Families last a long time and keep going even though
the people in them sometimes *change*.

Changes like:

New Babies   *New Husbands*

New Wives   *Aunts & Uncles*

Grandparents   *People move in and out.*

A Family Is...

a group of people who listen, who encourage, who care, and who share experiences.

Family Names

THERE ARE LOTS OF DIFFERENT NAMES FOR FAMILIES:

Nuclear
Extended
Blended
Single Parent
Kinship/Grandparent
Foster
Adopted
Childless

THESE NAMES ARE NOT WHAT ARE IMPORTANT BECAUSE ALL OF THESE TYPES OF FAMILIES HAVE SOME THINGS IN COMMON. THESE THINGS ARE:

They share experiences

They encourage each other

They listen

They care

How do families do these things?
What are some examples?

SIMON SAYS: "WHO'S IN YOUR FAMILY?"

Explain to the students that they will be playing a version of the game Simon Says, in which only some students will react to each command. Tell the students that they must watch carefully as they play the game because at the end you will be calling on some students to share one new thing they learned about a classmate. Lead the game of Simon Says:

o   Simon Says: "Everyone with a large family, stand up" (large being more than 4 people)

o   Simon Says: "Everyone with a family pet that is a dog, jump up and down."

o   Simon Says: "Everyone whose family has only two people in it, stand on one leg."

o   Simon Says: "Everyone, whose family looks alike, put their hands on their head."

o   Simon Says: "Everyone whose family has a stepmom or stepdad, rub your nose."

o   Simon Says: "Everyone whose family has a grandparent, aunt or uncle living with them, skip in a circle."

o   Simon Says: "Everyone who has someone in their family who was adopted, run in place."

o   Simon Says: "Everyone who has a family with one parent instead of two hop from side to side."

o   Simon Says: "Everyone whose family likes to be noisy rub your tummy."

o   Simon Says: "Everyone whose family cares about them, say" Yes, Yes, Yes!"

* Remember to give a direction without saying Simon Says to catch those not paying attention.*

Pass It On—Activity Game

MATERIALS NEEDED

An item to pass around the class like a bean bag, rubber snake or a stuffed animal. Game questions on cards.

INSTRUCTIONS

The object of the game is to pass the game prop on! To begin the game, have all the students stand in a circle. Select one person to be "it." That person holds the "game prop." You are the game "caller." You will say to the person holding the "game prop," "Name five places a family may visit, Pass it On!" This student passes the "game prop" to the right. And the other students pass the "game prop" as quickly as they can around the circle. If it returns to the original holder before they can name all five places, they are still "it." Whoever is holding the "game prop" when the person finishes naming the items is the next "it."

QUESTIONS TO ASK:

Name five places a family may visit.

Name three ways to say mother.

Name five pets a family might have.

Name three people you are related to that may live in your home.

What do we call your mother and father's sisters and brothers? (Aunts & Uncles)

Name three ways to say father.

Name five places to go on vacation.

Name five places where a family might like to eat.

Name five family celebrations (birthday, Passover, 4th of July, etc.)

Name three female family members. Not their names like Susie, but what are their roles in the family. (Sister, Mom, Aunt, Grandmother, Great-grandmother, etc.)

Name five chores families have to do.

Name five sports children in the family may play.

Name three jobs your mom has at home.

Name three jobs your father has at home.

Name three places an older brother or sister might work.

Name five games families may play at home.

Name five describing words that might be used to describe your family.

Name five things your family does for you.

Name three hobbies people in a family might have.

Name three traditions your family has (eating grilled cheese sandwiches and tomato soup on Sunday evening)

Activities About Family

Introducing My Family!

MATERIALS NEEDED

White paper, crayons or colored pencils. On the white paper you have printed at the top "Introducing My Family!"

Instruct the students to draw a family portrait. Under each family member's name write a word or two that describes them. You may draw your pets, too since they are an important part of your family.

What Is a Family?

MATERIALS NEEDED

Video Camera, Students, definitions of a family.

Have students think about what their definition of a family is. Make a recording of students in your class giving their definitions. You could also have the class sing the song "We Are Family," music and lyrics by Bernard Edwards, Nile Rogers. Share the video at the next school assembly or parent night.

Describing My Family

CIRCLE THE WORDS BELOW THAT BEST DESCRIBE YOUR FAMILY:

Loud	Fun	Like to Play Games	Funny	Loving
Noisy	Old	Outspoken	Young	Quiet
Honest	Tactful	Humorous	Serious	Warm
Caring	Small	Affectionate	Works	Encourage
Athletic	Artistic	Creative	Boring	Readers
Creative	Large	Like Sports	Kind	Collectors
Clean	Love	Thoughtful	Busy	Religious
Alike	Musical	Different Colors	Messy	Support
Blended	Big	Two Parent	Divorced	Comfort

There are lots of words we can use to describe our family!
Families come in all shapes, sizes and types!
Lots of different people can make up your family!

Family Matters

ANSWER THE FOLLOWING QUESTIONS ABOUT YOUR FAMILY:

1. What do you like best about each member of your family?_____

    _____

2. Do you try to be like your parents or different? _____

3. What are three describing words your family would use to describe you?

    _____   _____   _____

4. What is the most embarrassing thing your family does?_____

    _____

5. What is the most important advice your family has given you?_____

    _____

6. When someone tells you that you are just like your mom or dad, do you like it?
    Why or why not? _____

7. In what ways do you think you will treat your children the same way you have been
    treated by your parent? _____

8. What is the most useless advice you parents have given you?_____

    _____

9. What do you think your parents worried about at your age?_____

    _____

10. What is the most important life lesson you learned living with your family?

    _____

Bulletin Board Idea & Bookmark

BULLETIN BOARD IDEA:

Use this quote from the lesson

A family is a group of people who listen, who encourage, who care, who share experiences.

Use cut outs of different family types in a circle around the quote

---

TEN Benefits of frequent family dinners for children:

The more often children and teens eat dinner with their families, the less likely they are to smoke, drink or use drugs. Compared to kids who have fewer than three family dinners per week, children and teens who have frequent family dinners are:

- At 70 percent lower risk for substance abuse

- Half as likely to try cigarettes

- Half as likely to be daily cigarette smokers

- Half as likely to try marijuana

- One third less likely to try alcohol

- Half as likely to get drunk monthly

- Likelier to get better grades in school

- Less likely to have friends who drink alcohol and use marijuana

- Likelier to have parents who take responsibility for teen drug use

- Almost 40 percent likelier to say future drug use will never happen

Source: The National Center on Addiction and Substance Abuse at Columbia University's report The Importance of Family Dinners III.

PROMOTING FAMILY MEALS

What you can do to promote dinnertime as family time:

- Start the pattern of family dinners when children are young.

- Encourage your children to create menu ideas and participate in meal preparation.

- Turn off the TV and let your answering machine answer calls during dinnertime.

- Talk about what happened in everyone's day: school, work, extracurricular activities or current events.

- Establish a routine to start and end each meal. Light candles, say grace or tell a story.

- After dinner play a board game or serve dessert to encourage the family to continue the conversation.

- Keep conversation positive and make sure everyone gets a chance to speak.

Source: The National Center on Addiction and Substance Abuse (CASA) at Columbia University

FAMILY DAY—A DAY TO EAT DINNER WITH YOUR CHILDREN™

FAMILY DAY—A DAY TO EAT DINNER WITH YOUR CHILDREN™ is a day that has become a nationwide effort for parental involvement as a way to reduce substance abuse in children and teens. FAMILY DAY—A DAY TO EAT DINNER WITH YOUR CHILDREN™ stresses the importance of regular family activities to promote parent-child communication. It also encourages regular family dining as a way to promote this. The National Center of Addiction and Substance Abuse (CASA) at Columbia University launched FAMILY DAY—A DAY TO EAT DINNER WITH YOUR CHILDREN™ as a yearly event to take place on the fourth Monday of each September. Since 2001 the President and the governors of numerous states and the mayors and executives of hundreds of cities and counties have proclaimed FAMILY DAY—A DAY TO EAT DINNER WITH YOUR CHILDREN™. Since 1996 CASA research has consistently shown that the more children eat dinner with their families, the less likely they are to abuse drugs, smoke or drink alcohol.

CASA research consistently shows that frequent family dinners make a difference in teens' lives. Compared to teens who have five to seven family dinners in a typical week, teens who dine with their families fewer than three nights in a typical week are two times likelier to have tried marijuana, more than twice as likely to have tried cigarettes and one and a half times likelier to have tried alcohol, according to CASA's The Importance of Family Dinners III. The report also found that frequent family dinners are also associated with higher academic performance. Teens who have dinner with their families five to seven times in a typical week are likelier to get mostly A's and B's in school compared to teens who dine with their families fewer than three times per week. Academic performance is associated with substance abuse risk; Teens who report receiving grades of C or lower are at twice the risk of substance abuse as those who report receiving all A's or A's and B's.

Scrambled Words

Name: _____ Class: _____ Date: _____

EACH LINE HAS ONE WORD THAT IS SCRAMBLED. UNSCRAMBLE THAT WORD.

1. rneaGahdrft   _ _ _ _ _ _ _ _ _ _ _

2. taehFr   _ _ _ _ _ _

3. poStrup   _ _ _ _ _ _ _

4. lncUe   _ _ _ _ _

5. nFu   _ _ _

6. ednGatrromh   _ _ _ _ _ _ _ _ _ _ _

7. Lvoe   _ _ _ _

8. sCoinu   _ _ _ _ _ _

9. uAtn   _ _ _ _

10. nrDnei   _ _ _ _ _ _

11. nigarC   _ _ _ _ _ _

12. liFyma   _ _ _ _ _ _

13. orMthe   _ _ _ _ _ _

SELECT YOUR ANSWERS FROM THE FOLLOWING WORDS.
ANSWERS CAN BE FOUND ON PAGE 98.

Caring	Love	Uncle	Aunt
Grandfather	Grandmother	Dinner	Family
Cousin	Mother	Fun	Support
Father			

Secret Code

Name: _____ Class: _____ Date: _____

DECODE THE WORD IN EACH LINE.

1. yvnoqp   _ _ _ _ _ _

2. yvtebi   _ _ _ _ _ _

3. woggbi   _ _ _ _ _ _

4. fivgwyvtebi   _ _ _ _ _ _ _ _ _ _ _

5. mviogf   _ _ _ _ _ _

6. ysg   _ _ _

7. mxsrog   _ _ _ _ _ _

8. sgmqb   _ _ _ _ _

9. vsgt   _ _ _ _

10. nxtebi   _ _ _ _ _ _

11. qxkb   _ _ _ _

12. fivgwnxtebi   _ _ _ _ _ _ _ _ _ _ _

13. rsaaxit   _ _ _ _ _ _ _

SECRET CODE:

a	b	c	d	e	f	g	h	i	j	k	l	m	n	o	p	q	r	s	t	u	v	w	x	y	z
p	e	x	w	h	g	n	j	r	b	v	k	c	m	i	y	l	s	u	t	q	a	d	o	f	z

SELECT YOUR ANSWERS FROM THE FOLLOWIN WORDS. THE ANSWERS CAN BE FOUND ON PAGE 98.

Support	Family	Caring	Uncle	Grandmother
Grandfather	Love	Dinner	Aunt	Mother
Father	Fun	Cousin		

Name: _____ Class: _____ Date: _____

TRY TO FIND THE HIDDEN WORDS.

```
J S A N T A F S N Z J N Z V N R
V M S D J W E M Z E U M X X R L
C O U S I N E L O V E U F Q P L
N T G R A N D M O T H E R R E F
J H C A R I N G I H S H V K M H
G E P F D F Q E T C Q I P L V V
R R B S C U C X R C A Z E N L I
A F F U U N C L E J I M O F C M
N U A A I P Q I Y D E L P T F Z
D I N T M O P B V Q K B T X C X
F O H T H I L O I I R S Y E W
A M F T H E L J R N E S I A U R
T A A Y U D R Y W T D X A E U E
H J V O Y H N W K B P V L B D C
E Z G N W C E W L S S J Z P J D
R Z M E L B W W A C T C K U H Z
```

SELECT FROM THE FOLLOWING WORDS. THE ANSWERS CAN BE FOUND ON PAGE 98.

Grandfather	Caring	Love	Cousin
Uncle	Aunt	Family	Father
Mother	Grandmother	Support	Fun
Dinner			

Answers

Scrambled Words page 95
1. Grandfather
2. Father
3. Support
4. Uncle
5. Fun
6. Grandmother
7. Love
8. Cousin
9. Aunt
10. Dinner
11. Caring
12. Family
13. Mother

Secret Code page 96
1. Family
2. Father
3. Dinner
4. Grandfather
5. Caring
6. Fun
7. Cousin
8. Uncle
9. Aunt
10. Mother
11. Love
12. Grandmother
13. Support

Word Search page 97

```
•  •  •  •  •  •  •  •  •  •  •  •  •  •  •
•  M  •  D  •  •  •  •  •  •  •  •  •  •  •
C  O  U  S  I  N  •  L  O  V  E  •  •  •  •
•  T  G  R  A  N  D  M  O  T  H  E  R  •  •
•  H  C  A  R  I  N  G  •  •  •  •  •  •  •
G  E  •  •  F  E  •  •  •  •  •  •  •  •  •
R  R  •  S  •  U  •  R  •  •  •  •  •  •  •
A  F  F  •  U  N  C  L  E  •  •  •  •  •  •
N  U  A  A  •  P  •  •  •  •  •  •  •  •  •
D  •  N  T  M  •  P  •  •  •  •  •  •  •  •
F  •  •  T  H  I  •  O  •  •  •  •  •  •  •
A  •  •  •  •  E  L  •  R  •  •  •  •  •  •
T  •  •  •  •  R  Y  •  T  •  •  •  •  •  •
H  •  •  •  •  •  •  •  •  •  •  •  •  •  •
E  •  •  •  •  •  •  •  •  •  •  •  •  •  •
R  •  •  •  •  •  •  •  •  •  •  •  •  •  •
```

Chapter Six

National Native American Indian and Alaska Native Heritage Month:

RESPONSIBILITY FOR THE EARTH

National Native American Indian Heritage Month

National Native American Indian Heritage Month honors many contributions and accomplishments of American Indians and Alaska Natives. They were the first people to call our country home. Throughout our history American Indian and Alaska Native people have been an integral part of American character. Against difficult odds they have endured, and they remain a vital cultural, political, social and moral presence in our country. Native Americans have brought to our country certain values and ideals that have been ingrained in the spirit of our country, like the knowledge that we can thrive and prosper without destroying the environment or the understanding that people from different cultures, backgrounds, religions and traditions can come together to build a great country. They bring the cultural awareness that diversity can be a resource, an asset rather than a divisive force.

There are some key events that led up to the establishment of National Native American Indian and Alaska Native Heritage Month. The proposals to honor Native Americans first started around the turn of the century. In 1914 Red Fox James, a member of the Blackfoot Tribe, rode horseback from state to state in hope of rounding up support for the tribute. In the following year a member of the Seneca tribe, Dr. Arthur C. Parker, was able to convince The Boy Scouts to establish a day of recognition for Native Americans. The first state to observe American Indian Day was New York, in 1916. Over the years many states followed their lead. In 1976 a resolution by the United States Senate declared the week of October 10-16 as Native American Awareness Week. The celebration was expanded to a month in 1990.

Oral traditions that pass wisdom and stories are an important part of Native American culture. Through the years this is the way many life lessons were taught. The respect and responsibility to protect and care for mother earth is a theme that has been handed down through the generations of Native Americans. In honor of National Native American Indian and Alaska Native Heritage Month our lesson is responsibility for the earth.

LESSON—RESPONSIBILITY FOR THE EARTH

OBJECTIVES:
🌳 At the end of the lesson the students will be able to explain the Native American views on taking care of the earth.

🌳 At the end of the lesson the students will be able to list three ways they may be more responsible for their actions in caring for the earth.

MATERIALS NEEDED:
overhead projector, overheads, and activity for lesson, story to share, follow up activity.

APPLAUSE FOR THIS LESSON:
"Awesome Applause"- Raise hands over heads, clap one time, bend at waist and bow down towards the floor and say "Awwwwesome." Because caring for the earth is "awesome!"

OPTIONAL MATERIALS:
Open the lesson with Native American music and play the music during the group activity. Suggested CD Canyon Trilogy: Native American Flute Music- R. Carlos Nakai

1. Open the lesson by sharing some information about National Native American Indian and Alaska Native Heritage Month. Adjust the information you share with the age of the students to whom you are presenting.

2. Do the lesson group activity. Reward with "Awesome Applause."

3. Use the overheads in the following order:

    🌳 Treat the earth

    🌳 Hold on to what is good

    🌳 Responsible people

    🌳 Responsibility looks like

    🌳 Many types of responsibility- Read your selected story after these overheads and ask the students which type of responsibility the story was about.

    🌳 How can I start being responsible?

    🌳 Responsibility is important

4. End the lesson by reminding the students this month would be a great time to check books out of the library to learn more about Native Americans who have many good things to teach us about caring for the earth.

Books

Native Americans: Let Our Words Be Heard—
  Peggy K. Ford

Gluskabe and the Four Wishes—retold by
  Joseph Bruchac

*Pushing Up the Sky Seven Native American
  Plays for Children*—Joseph Bruchac

Ma'ii and Cousin Horned Toad—Shonto Begay

Clamshell Boy—Written and adapted by Terri
  Cohlene

The Quillworker a Cheyenne Legend—written
  and adapted by Terri Cohlene

*In a Circle Long Ago: A Treasury of Native Lore
  from North America*—N. Van Laan

*Fire Race: A Karuk Coyote Tale About How Fire
  Came to People*—Jonathan London

Beyond the Ridge—Paul Goble

Brave Bear and the Ghosts a Sioux Legend—
  Retold by Gloria Dominic

Coyote and the Grasshoppers A Pomo Legend—
  retold by Gloria Dominic

*First Woman and the Strawberry a Cherokee
  Legend*—retold by Gloria Dominic.

Katie Henio: Navajo Sheepherder—Peggy
  Thompson

Fox Song—Joseph Bruchac

*The White Deer and Other Stories Told by the
  Lenape*—John Bierhorst

Activity Lesson: Native American Wisdom

Divide the students into groups and have them sit in a circle in their groups. A circle symbolizes support and unity with other group members, and everyone has an equal seat in the group. Assign each group a Native American tribe name. This will also be the source of the group's proverb or quote to be interpreted. Each group will answer the questions listed below and report back to the class. Groups will be: Navajo tribe, Makah tribe, Cheyenne tribe, Shawnee tribe, Pomo tribe and Zuni tribe. *Play optional Native American music during group time.*

1. What does this quote mean?

2. What does it advise you to do? How should you go about doing this?

3. What character principle does it talk about? (Citizenship, Caring, Fairness, Respect or Responsibility)

4. Describe in your report to the class the important facts about the tribe.

"I see the Earth.
I am looking at Her and smile.
Because She makes me happy.
The Earth, looking back at me
Is smiling too.
May I walk happily
And lightly
Upon Her."
NAVAJO CHANT

The Navajo called themselves "Dinneh," which means "The People." The word Navajo comes from the Pueblo word "navahu" which means planters of huge fields. Often there was not enough water to raise good crops, and sometimes there was flash flooding. Often they moved from one home (hogan) in the desert to another one in the mountains. They are the largest tribe in the United States and are related to the native people of Alaska and Canada. They lived in the areas we now call Arizona and New Mexico.

"I dance because I am rich."
MAKAH CHIEFTAIN

The Makah lived along the Pacific Northwest Coast, near what is now known as Washington State. They called themselves "Kweedishchaaht," meaning, "People of the Cape." This tribe was especially skilled at hunting whales. They were one of the few people who hunted whales at sea. They were also excellent craftsmen. They were able to make tools to allow them to cut planks for houses, and to make bentwood boxes, weaving looms, ceremonial masks and canoes.

Native American Wisdom

*"As you go forward into your life,
You will come upon a great chasm.
Jump. It is not as wide as you think."*
ZUNI

The Zuni called the home where they lived "The Middle Place." For centuries this has been near the Rio Grande River in New Mexico close to the border of Arizona. They along with their neighbors the Acoma, the Hopi and others were known as Pueblos. Pueblo is a Spanish term which means village or town and also refers to the multi-leveled, apartment-like structures they live in. They were desert farmers; both men and women grew crops with special watering techniques. Both sexes shared the repair of their building and home. Women owned property and when a man married, he moved into his wife's home or mother-in-law's home.

*"Nothing lives long
Only the earth
And the mountains."*
CHEYENNE SONG

The Cheyenne people lived in earth lodges near Lake Superior. They lived in a fertile area and raised crops and the men often did not need to hunt. After the Spanish explorers introduced them to horses, they gave up their permanent village home to follow the buffalo herds on the Great Plains. On the Great Plains they lived in tipi villages that could be easily moved. A tipi is made of long sturdy poles and covered with buffalo skins.

"Sell a country! Why not sell the air, the great sea, as well as the earth?"
TECUMSEH, SHAWNEE

The Shawnee were nomads. This means they were always on the move. Villages regularly broke into smaller groups to flee from attacking tribes or to search for better farming ground. Different bands lived in various states including Alabama, Georgia and Pennsylvania. They had moved to the Ohio Valley and Kentucky areas by the 17th century. One of their greatest war chiefs was Tecumseh. He worked hard to unite the tribes to fight against encroaching white settlers. He was a gifted warrior, leader and speaker.

*"What is a man? A man is nothing.
Without his family he is of less importance than that bug crossing a trail."*
ANONYMOUS (POMO), 1944

The Pomo homeland was north of San Francisco Bay and across the central region of California. Families lived in the same area generation after generation and harvested from the same trees generation after generation. They spoke seven related languages. They were hunter-gatherers; the men hunted and the women gathered food from the area. The Pomos were known for their beautiful baskets. Both men and women were accomplished basket weavers. The baskets were decorated with shells, beads and tiny colorful feathers.

"Treat the earth well: it was not given to you by your parents, it was loaned to you by your children. We do not inherit the Earth from our Ancestors, we borrow it from our Children."

QUESTIONS:

WHAT DOES IT MEAN TO BE RESPONSIBLE FOR SOMETHING?

It's like you are in charge.

It is your job to take care of something.

HOW DOES RESPONSIBILITY RELATE TO THIS ANCIENT INDIAN PROVERB?

A Pueblo Indian Prayer

Hold on to what is good,
Even if it's a handful of earth.

Hold on to what you believe,
Even if it's a tree that stands by itself.

Hold on to what you must do,
Even if it is a long way from here.

Hold on to your life,
Even if it is easier to let go.

Hold on to my hand,
Even if someday I'll be
gone away from you.

QUESTION:

HOW IS RESPONSIBILITY EXPLAINED
IN THIS PUEBLO INDIAN PRAYER?

Responsible People...

Fix their mistakes.

Do what they are supposed to do,
when they are supposed to do it.

Keep on trying even when it is hard.

Are self-disciplined
That means they are able to give up what they
really want to do and do what needs to get done.

They stop and think before they act.
They consider the consequences.

Responsibility Looks Like...

You complete your assignments on time.

If you make a mistake you admit it.

You complete your chores on time.

No blaming mistakes on others — you try to fix them.

Picking up trash.

Three R's — Reuse, Reduce, Recycle

Returning things you borrow to others and the earth.

Taking care of your pet and other living creatures.

You follow through without giving up.

"Humankind has not
woven the web of life,
we are but one thread within it.
Whatever we do to the web,
we do to ourselves.
All things connect."

—Chief Seattle, 1854

Types of Responsibility

THERE ARE MANY TYPES OF RESPONSIBILITY:

MORAL RESPONSIBILITY

To the earth and everything in it. People and animals too.
To care, help, defend, build, preserve and honor.

"As you go forward into your life,
you will come upon a great chasm.
Jump. It is not as wide as you think."
—Zuni tribe

LEGAL RESPONSIBILITY

To the rules, laws and ordinances in your classroom,
school, community and country. If there is a rule or
law that is discriminatory you work to fix it.

"Sell a country! Why not sell the air,
the great sea, as well as the earth?"
—Tecumseh, Shawnee

FAMILY RESPONSIBILITY

Treating the members of your family with love, respect and dignity.

"What is a man? A man is nothing.
Without his family he is of less importance
than that bug crossing a trail."
—Anonymous (Pomo tribe), 1944

How Can I Start Being Responsible?

Follow through on assignments, chores and responsibilities to self and others.

Practice self control the next time you are angry.

Clean up your area after lunch; pick up trash, help your family recycle.

Express your feelings with appropriate words and actions.

Keep your word to yourself and others.

Keep a promise even when it is hard.

Remember your actions affect people and our world.

Responsibility is Important

Because...

It is essential for keeping our wonderful earth a good place to live.

"When all the trees have been cut down,
when all the animals have been hunted,
when all the waters are polluted,
when all the air is unsafe to breathe,
only then will you discover you cannot eat money."
—Cree Prophecy

"I do not think the measure of a civilization
is how tall its buildings of concrete are,
but rather how well its people have learned
to relate to their environment and fellow man."
—Sun Bear of the Chippewa Tribe

Craft Activity: Dream Catcher

Woodland Indians hung dream catchers near windows in their lodges to catch all dreams. The teaching says that all bad dreams would be caught in the catcher's webbing until morning when the sunlight would burn them off and the night's good dreams would be caught in the feathers to be dreamed another night. Many people use dream catchers still today for their tradition and beauty.

MATERIALS:

Round paper plate to be used as the template, construction paper in assorted colors, yarn or string, feathers, scissors, glue, newspaper, ribbon, white paint and aluminum pie pans

INSTRUCTIONS:

- Have students trace around the paper plate on the construction paper to make the circle.

- Students will cut a few lengths of string or yarn slightly longer than the circle diameter.

- On the table that you have spread with newspaper, the students will dip their lengths of string into paint and lay the strings across the circle to make a pattern or web. Then gently pick up the string and discard in waste basket.

- After the paint dries glue a few clean lengths of string or yarn to the bottom of the dream catcher. Attach feathers to bottom after glue has dried.

- Slip a ribbon through the hole at the top of the dream catcher and tie the ribbon.

NATIVE AMERICAN INDIAN AND
ALASKA HERITAGE MONTH

MATERIALS NEEDED:
Blue paper or fabric to cover board, complementary border, cut out of earth, black or white letters quote printed in large font on your computer.

INSTRUCTIONS:
- Cover the Bulletin Board with blue paper/fabric

- Use a large cut out of the earth, attach

- In letters say -Native American Indian and Alaska Native Heritage Month

- Attach the quote

> "Treat the earth well:
> it was not given to you
> by your parents,
> it was loaned to you
> by your children.
>
> We do not inherit
> the Earth from
> our Ancestors;
> we borrow it
> from our Children."
>
> *Ancient Indian Proverb*

NATIVE AMERICAN HERITAGE

National American Indian Heritage Month honors many contributions and accomplishments of American Indians and Alaska Natives. They were the first people to call our country home. Throughout our history American Indian and Alaska Native people have been an integral part of American character. Against difficult odds they have endured, and they remain a vital cultural, political, social and moral presence in our country. Native Americans have brought to our country certain values and ideals that have been ingrained in the spirit of our country, like the knowledge that we can thrive and prosper without destroying the environment or the understanding that people from different cultures, backgrounds, religions and traditions can come together to build a great country. They bring the cultural awareness that diversity can be a resource, an asset rather than a divisive force.

There are some key events that led up to the establishment of National Native American Indian and Alaska Native Heritage Month. The proposals to honor Native Americans first started around the turn of the century. In 1914 Red Fox James, a member of the Blackfoot Tribe, rode horseback from state to state in hope of rounding up support for the tribute. In the following year a member of the Seneca tribe, Dr. Arthur C. Parker, was able to convince The Boy Scouts to establish a day of recognition for Native Americans. The first state to observe American Indian Day was New York, in 1916. Over the years many states followed their lead. In 1976 a resolution by the United States Senate declared the week of October 10-16 as Native American Awareness Week. The celebration was expanded to a month in 1990.

"Treat the earth well: it was not given to you by your parents, it was loaned to you by your children.

We do not inherit the Earth from our Ancestors; we borrow it from our Children."

Ancient Indian Proverb

Mix and Match

NATIVE AMERICAN PROVERBS AND QUOTES

Name: _____ Class: _____ Date: _____

FILL IN THE BLANK WITH THE LETTER NEXT TO THE WORD THAT BEST COMPLETES THE SENTENCE.

1. "As you go _____ into your life, you will come upon a great chasm. Jump.
   It is not as wide as you think." —Zuni tribe

2. "When all trees have been cut down, when all the animals have been hunted,
   when all the waters are _____, when all the air is unsafe to breathe, only then
   will you discover you cannot eat money." —Cree Prophecy

3. "Treat the Earth well: it was not given to you by your parents, it was loaned to you
   by your children. We do not inherit the Earth from our _____, we borrow it from
   our Children." —Ancient Indian Proverb

4. "Hold on to what is good even if it is a _____ of the earth." —Pueblo Indian Prayer

5. "Sell a country! Why not sell the air, the great sea, as well as the _____?" —Tecumseh, Shawnee

6. "I do not think the measure of a civilization is how tall its buildings of concrete are,
   but rather how well its people have learned to relate to their _____ and fellow man."
   —Sun Bear of the Chippewa Tribe

7. "What is a man? A man is nothing. WIthout his family he is of less _____ than
   that bug crossing a trail." —Anonymous Pomo tribe, 1944

8. "Humankind has not woven the thread of _____ we are but one thread within it.
   Whatever we do to the web, we do to ourselves. All things connect." Chief Seattle, 1854

9. "Hold on to what you believe, even it it's a tree that stands by _____." —Pueblo Indian Prayer

SELECT YOUR ANSWERS FROM THE FOLLOWING WORDS.
ANSWERS CAN BE FOUND ON PAGE 118.

a. polluted	d. forward	g. earth
b. handful	e. itself	h. environment
c. life	f. Ancestors:	i. importance

NATIVE AMERICAN PROVERBS AND QUOTES

Name: _____Class:_____Date: _____

DECODE THE WORD IN EACH SENTENCE.

1. "Sell a country! Why not sell the air, the great sea, as well as the _ _ _ _ _?" —Tecumseh, Shawnee **(hxjvp)**

2. "When all trees have been cut down, when all the animals have been hunted, when all the waters are – – – – – – – –, when all the air is unsafe to breathe, only then will you discover you cannot eat money." —Cree Prophecy **(wunnavhr)**

3. "I do not think the measure of a civilization is how tall its buildings of concrete are, but rather how well its people have learned to relate to their _ _ _ _ _ _ _ _ _ _ _ and fellow man." —Sun Bear of the Chippewa Tribe **(hegmjuezhev)**

4. "As you go _ _ _ _ _ _ _ into your life, you will come upon a great chasm. Jump. It is not as wide as you think." —Zuni tribe **(sujcxjr)**

5. "What is a man? A man is nothing. WIthout his family he is of less _ _ _ _ _ _ _ _ _ _ than that bug crossing a trail." —Anonymous Pomo tribe, 1944 **(mzwujvxeth)**

6. "Hold on to what you believe, even it it's a tree that stands by _ _ _ _ _ _." —Pueblo Indian Prayer **(mvyhns)**

7. "Treat the Earth well: it was not given to you by your parents, it was loaned to you by your children. We do not inherit the Earth from our _ _ _ _ _ _ _ _ _, we borrow it from our Children." —Ancient Indian Proverb **(xethyvujy)**

8. "Humankind has not woven the thread of _ _ _ _ we are but one thread within it. Whatever we do to the web, we do to ourselves. All things connect." Chief Seattle, 1854 **(nmsh)**

9. "Hold on to what is good even if it is a _ _ _ _ _ _ _ of the earth." —Pueblo Indian Prayer **(pxersan)**

SECRET CODE:

a b c d e f g h i j k l m n o p q r s t u v w x y z
u z w k n j v e x r y q i l g h b d f c o t p a s

SELECT YOUR ANSWERS FROM THE FOLLOWING WORDS.
ANSWERS CAN BE FOUND ON PAGE 118.

polluted	earth	life
itself	forward	environment
Ancestors;	importance	handful

Crossword Puzzle

NATIVE AMERICAN PROVERBS AND QUOTES

Name: _____ Class: _____ Date: _____

FILL IN THE CROSSWORD PUZZLE BY USING THE CLUES.

ACROSS:

1. "Hold on to what is good even if it is a _ _ _ _ _ _ _ of the earth." —Pueblo Indian Prayer

2. "Humankind has not woven the thread of _ _ _ _ we are but one thread within it. Whatever we do to the web, we do to ourselves. All things connect." Chief Seattle, 1854

3. "As you go _ _ _ _ _ _ _ into your life, you will come upon a great chasm. Jump. It is not as wide as you think." —Zuni tribe

4. "What is a man? A man is nothing. WIthout his family he is of less _ _ _ _ _ _ _ _ _ _ than that bug crossing a trail." —Anonymous Pomo tribe, 1944

5. "Hold on to what you believe, even if it's a tree that stands by _ _ _ _ _ _." —Pueblo Indian Prayer

DOWN:

1. "I do not think the measure of a civilization is how tall its buildings of concrete are, but rather how well its people have learned to relate to their _ _ _ _ _ _ _ _ _ _ and fellow man." —Sun Bear of the Chippewa Tribe

2. "Treat the Earth well: it was not given to you by your parents, it was loaned to you by your children. We do not inherit the Earth from our _ _ _ _ _ _ _ _ _, we borrow it from our Children." —Ancient Indian Proverb

3. "When all trees have been cut down, when all the animals have been hunted, when all the waters are – – – – – – – –, when all the air is unsafe to breathe, only then will you discover you cannot eat money." —Cree Prophecy

4. "Sell a country! Why not sell the air, the great sea, as well as the _ _ _ _ _?" —Tecumseh, Shawnee

SELECT YOUR ANSWERS FROM THE FOLLOWING WORDS. ANSWERS CAN BE FOUND ON PAGE 118.

importance	polluted	earth
forward	handful	environment
life	itself	Ancestors;

Answers:

Mix and Match page 115.
1. d. forward
2. a. polluted
3. f. Ancestors;
4. b. handful
5. g. earth
6. h. environment
7. i. importance
8. c. life
9. e. itself

Secret Code page 116
1. earth
2. polluted
3. environment
4. forward
5. importance
6. itself
7. Ancestors;
8. life
9. handful

Crossword Puzzle on page 117

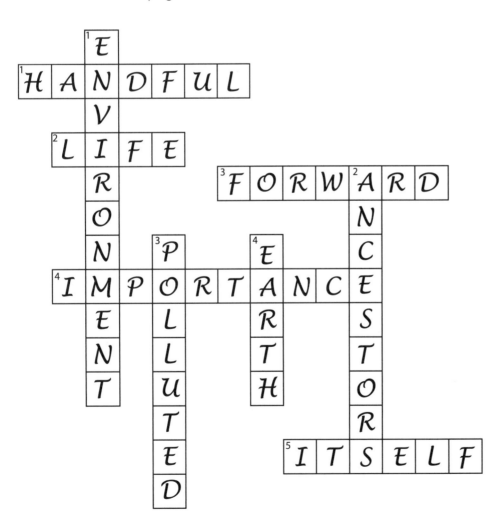

Chapter Seven

The Olympic Games, Super Bowl, NCAA Playoffs and the World Series

SPORTSMANSHIP

Sportsmanship

THE OLYMPIC GAMES, SUPER BOWL, NCAA PLAYOFFS AND THE WORLD SERIES

The Olympic Games, Super Bowl, NCAA Playoffs and the World Series bring out the sports enthusiasm in many of us, whether it is watching the Super Bowl to see the creative commercials that companies have spent millions of dollars to create or watching the gifted athletes on the field. NCAA Playoffs are so popular that they have earned the name March Madness, and office pools are formed with friendly wagering to speculate on team favorites. And the World Series is closely scrutinized by the fans of the American and National baseball leagues. If you can't beat them, why not join them where their interests are during this time of the year? The lesson for this unit is sportsmanship. Sportsmanship is something that can be practiced both inside and outside of the classroom. Sportsmanship is something we hope to see the athletes practice during these important games.

THE SUPER BOWL

The Super Bowl is the National Football League (NFL) championship game. In professional American football, it is the biggest game of the season. The game and all of the festivities surrounding it constitute "Super Bowl Sunday." Many popular musicians and singers have performed during the pre-game and half-time ceremonies. Super Bowl Sunday is the second-largest day of food consumption behind Thanksgiving (American Institute of Food Distribution). The location of the Super Bowl is chosen by the NFL well in advance, usually 3 to 5 years before the game. Cities compete to host the game in a selection bidding simi-

lar to ones used by soccer's World Cup and the Olympics. The Super Bowl is one of the most watched broadcasts of the year. Because of this many companies spend millions of dollars on commercials to be broadcast on the program. The game began in January, 1967, as the AFL-NFL World Championship Game in which the NFL championship team played against the championship team of the American Football League (AFL) for the "World Championship of Professional Football." After both leagues merged in 1970, the Super Bowl became known as the NFL's championship game. Since then the game has been played each year the Sunday after the playoffs.

NCAA PLAYOFFS

"March Madness," or the Big Dance, has become one of the United States most prominent sports events. The famous basketball tournaments last for 20 days. The participants include regional champions and other top teams. It is set up as a single elimination format. The event first started in 1939 and has a tradition that has included dramatic wins by underdog teams and outstanding performances of reigning winning teams. The tournament bracket is made up of champions from each Division I conference, which will receive automatic bids. The other slots are at-large berths, with teams chosen by the selection committee of the NCAA. The term Elite Eight refers to the final eight teams in the NCAA Division I Men's or Women's Basketball Championship. The Elite Eight consists of the teams in the final game of each of the four regional brackets. The NCAA Playoffs is a popular event for office pools and wagers.

THE OLYMPICS

The Olympic Games are an international multi-sports event that takes place every four years. They are made up of summer and winter games. Originally held in ancient Greece, these games were revived in the late 19th century. The summer games have been held every fourth year starting in 1896, with the exception of the years during the World Wars. A special edition for winter sports, the Olympic Winter Games, was held first in 1924. The first winter Olympics were held as a non-Olympic sports festival. They were declared to be the official Games by the International Olympic Committee in 1925. Originally both summer and winter games were held in the same year but that changed in 1994. Since then the Winter Games and the Summer Games have been held two years apart. The Olympic Flame has been lit since the 1928 Summer Olympics, but the torch relay did not start until 1936. The opening and closing ceremonies of the Olympics combine traditional elements with celebration, artistic displays and dance.

The five Olympic rings that are intertwined represent unity of the five continents. The rings appear in five colors on a white field. The colors are red, blue, green, yellow and black. These colors were chosen because each nation had at least one of these colors in its national flag.

The Olympic motto is "Citius, Altius, Fortius," a Latin phrase meaning "Swifter, Higher, Stronger."

The Olympic Creed: "The most important thing in the Olympic Games is not to win but to take part, just as the most important thing in life is not triumph but the struggle. The essential thing is not to have conquered but to have fought well."

THE WORLD SERIES

The postseason playoff series between the champions of the two major professional baseball leagues in the United States, the American League and the National League, is a hot ticket to have and a favorite to watch on television, especially if your local or favorite team is competing. The World Series began in 1903 after the hostilities ended between the National League and the newly formed American League. The seven-game format has been a standard since 1922. Beginning in 1955, one player has been voted the Most Valuable Player of each series, a coveted honor in baseball. The World Series term has also been applied to several baseball championships the Junior World Series played between the International League and the American Association (both professional minor leagues); and the Little League World Series, which is an annual international event for teams of boys and girls 9-18 years old.

LESSON—SPORTSMANSHIP

OBJECTIVES:

- ⚽ At the end of the lesson the students will be able to explain two facts concerning the Super Bowl or the NCAA Playoffs.

- ⚽ At the end of the lesson the students will be able to explain three ways to practice good sportsmanship.

- ⚽ At the end of the lesson students will be able to explain how sportsmanship is important both inside and outside of the classroom.

MATERIALS NEEDED:

Overheads, story, materials for activity "Let's Practice Sportsmanship." Sportsmanship Checklist for Kids- a copy for each student.

"HIGH FIVE APPLAUSE":

Clap hands over head once and then bring your hand over to the hand of the person next to you and give a high five. Why High Five Applause? Because it is a way to say "good job," or "way to go;" and practicing good sportsmanship is always a good way to go.

1. Start the lesson by talking about either the Super Bowl or NCAA Playoffs giving background information that is appropriate to the age level of students you are teaching. Ask the students if the players in these famous games practice good sportsmanship. Use High Five Applause to reward the students.

2. Introduce the lesson by saying today we are going to learn about good sportsmanship, and it is something that can be practiced both inside and outside of the classroom. Then ask the students, "What is good sportsmanship? Can you give me an example of it?" Use High Five Applause to reward the students.

3. Have the students do the self inventory Sportsmanship Checklist for Kids. Allow time for completion. Tell students the sometimes answers and never answers are areas they might want to work on improving.

4. Then tell the students they can follow along on the checklist as you use the overheads to see how they can improve. Use the overheads in the following order:

- ⚽ Sportsmanship is.....

- ⚽ Sportsmanship checklist

5. Read the selected story to the class, and after the story talk about who practiced good sportsmanship and who did not.

6. Use the application activity "Let's Practice Sportsmanship." Use High Five Applause to reward the students.

7. End the lesson by reminding the students good sportsmanship can be practiced both inside and outside of the classroom. And tell them you hope their favorite teams win!

You're a Good Sport, Miss Malarkey—Judy Finchler

The Real Winner—Charise Neugebauer

The Babe & I—David Adler

Goal—Robert Burleigh

Agnes Plays Soccer: A Cow's Lesson in Sportsmanship—Wendy Potratz

A Team of One—Ila Wallen

Jackie Robinson—Kenneth Rudeen

The Berenstain Bears Go Out for the Team—Stan and Jan Berenstain

Backyard Basketball Superstar—Monica Klein

S.O.R. Losers—by Avi

Soccer Duel—Thomas Dygard

Boulden Publishing: *Sportsmanship Playing the Game*—Video & CD-ROM

Buddy Learns to Play Fair—Video & CD-ROM

Sportsmanship is...

- 🏈 The ability to win or do well without bragging, gloating or rubbing it in.

- 🏈 The ability to lose without making excuses, blaming or complaining.

- 🏈 The ability to forgive yourself when you make a mistake and not pout, blame others or make excuses. Learn from the mistake and be ready to continue.

- 🏈 If someone you are playing or working with makes a mistake, don't criticize but encourage. Criticizing just takes the focus off of what you are trying to accomplish.

- 🏈 Treat with respect the project or game as well as teammates, group members, teachers, and coaches.

Sportsmanship Check List

I TRY TO AVOID ARGUMENTS-

🏈 Anger management is important.

🏈 Anger can affect performance when you need to stay focused.

🏈 Letting off steam and yelling at people can be a bad habit.

I ALWAYS FOLLOW THE RULES IN GAMES AND GROUP WORK.

🏈 It is your responsibility to know the rules and abide by them.

🏈 It is your responsibility to do your part but not everyone else's.

I SHARE RESPONSIBILITIES WITH THOSE I WORK AND PLAY WITH.

🏈 Your behavior affects everyone on the team and in the group.

🏈 Do your share and encourage others;
they have a responsibility to do the same.

Sportsmanship Check List

I GIVE EVERYONE A CHANCE TO PARTICIPATE.

- You need to encourage everyone to participate, not just the gifted people.

- Nobody likes a show off or just one person doing all the work.

I RESPECT OTHER PEOPLE'S EFFORTS.

- Whether one person is better than another is not important. What is important is that you encourage everyone to be the best they can be.

- If you do better than someone else, don't gloat, show off or belittle someone else who didn't do as well.

I ACCEPT JUDGMENT CALLS OF TEACHERS AND GAME OFFICIALS.

- Don't argue. Accept the decision. Then refocus back on the project or the game and do your best!

I ENCOURAGE PEOPLE I WORK WITH.

- Praise those you work with when they do well. This builds confidence.

- Comfort and encourage those who make mistakes. This builds self-esteem.

- People work much better with praise, comfort and encouragement than with criticism. Criticism makes you feel there is something wrong with you.

Sportsmanship Check List

I HAVE GOOD LISTENING SKILLS.

🏈 When teachers or coaches give directions, look at them, think about what they are saying and ask questions if you don't understand.

🏈 If you disagree, do it privately and not in front of the whole group.

I ALWAYS PLAY FAIR INSIDE AND OUTSIDE OF THE CLASSROOM.

🏈 Honesty and integrity never go out of style.

🏈 A good grade or a win by cheating is not a victory or something to be celebrated.

I END THE GAME OR GROUP SMOOTHLY.

🏈 When the project is over regardless of the outcome, no pouting, blaming, threatening or trying to change the results.

🏈 Congratulate other groups or teams for a job well done.

🏈 Encourage other teams or group members if the outcome was not what you'd anticipated. Congratulate them if it went well on a job well done, whether it turned out well for you or not.

Activity Lesson: "Let's Practice Sportsmanship!"

OBJECTIVE:

Students will draw a situation out of the container, read it to the class, and then respond by practicing good sportsmanship. Reward the student for his or her participation with High Five Applause.

"HIGH FIVE APPLAUSE":

Clap hands over head once and then bring your hand to meet the hand of the person next to you and give a high five.

MATERIALS NEEDED:

Ellison Die cuts of sports related objects like gym shoes, baseball bats, footballs etc. Assorted construction paper, glue. Sport container to hold situations cards.(Halloween is a good time to look for sports related Trick or Treat Bags that could be used)

(Alternative to using Ellison Die cuts would be to purchase sports egg containers that look like Easter eggs but are soccer balls, footballs, etc. Put situations inside of them. Still laminate the statements so they last longer.)

INSTRUCTIONS:

- Select from the examples on page 127 of sportsmanship.

- Glue them to Ellison die cuts

- Laminate

Your group was not selected for the talent show at school. Everyone is really disappointed. You all practiced very hard. What do you do?

- -

You didn't get the important part you wanted in the class Thanksgiving Play. You have been put in charge of the scenery and props. What do you do?

- -

The bases are loaded. It is the end of the ninth, and your best friend is up to bat. They strike out. This means you lost the game and a chance to go to play-offs. What do you do?

- -

You didn't get chosen for the select soccer team. You practiced every evening and weekend for the past three months. But your next door neighbor made the team. What do you do?

- -

Your group has worked really hard on the project your teacher assigned. For once everyone in the group did his or her part and they did a good job. You present your project to the class, and the teacher asks so many questions that you are not sure whether it is still good or not. What do you do?

- -

You are on a select basketball team. At recess you like to shoot hoops. It is fun. You also try to give pointers to everyone on how to improve their shots. But today you notice people whispering and looking at each other when you try to teach them to do better. What should you do?

- -

Your skit was accepted for the Red Ribbon Day program. Your group is excited. But when you are timing the skit, it is one minute too long. What should you do?

- -

You have been put in a group to work on a class project. It is the worst group you have ever been in! What was the teacher thinking? No one in the group is talking; everyone is just looking at each other. All the other groups in class have gotten started. What should you do?

- -

Your game has been stopped because the quarterback on the other team has been hurt. You thought he was behaving like a jerk anyway and showing off when he threw the ball. Some of your teammates said he deserved to be hurt, the showoff! What should you do?

- -

At the science fair you got second place. You thought you had done the best project ever! You had put so much work into it. The person who got first is on your bus. You will see her tomorrow. What should you do?

Activity: Create a Game Plan

All successful teams and coaches have a game plan. Have the students create a Game Plan for practicing sportsmanship both inside and outside of the classroom. Display the game plan on a giant clipboard that you have made.

MATERIALS NEEDED:
One large piece of poster board, black marker, bulletin board paper for border, construction paper for clip.

INSTRUCTIONS:
- Create a giant clipboard from a piece of poster board.

- Using a black marker, create lines on the poster board for writing the game plan.

- Add a border that is two inches larger than the poster board. Create the border out of bulletin board paper.

- Create a clip for the top of the clipboard, write Game Plan on the clip and attach with glue.

- When the game plan has been created, laminate and display it in the classroom or hallway.

Here is a suggestion on what a game plan for good sportsmanship might look like:

- **No Bragging or showing off.**

- **Lose without complaining**

- **Encourage, don't criticize.**

- **Forgive mistakes.**

- **Respect the game or project.**

- **No arguments.**

- **Play by the rules.**

- **Share responsibilities.**

- **Give everyone a chance.**

Sportsmanship Checklist for Kids

RATE YOURSELF IN THE FOLLOWING CATEGORIES.

I try to avoid arguments	Always	Sometimes	Never
I always follow the rules in games and group work.	Always	Sometimes	Never
I share responsibilities with those I work and play with.	Always	Sometimes	Never
I give everyone a chance to participate.	Always	Sometimes	Never
I respect other people's efforts.	Always	Sometimes	Never
I accept judgment calls of teachers and game officials.	Always	Sometimes	Never
I encourage people I work with.	Always	Sometimes	Never
I have good listening skills.	Always	Sometimes	Never
I always play fair inside and outside of the classroom.	Always	Sometimes	Never
I end the game or group smoothly.	Always	Sometimes	Never

SOMETIMES AND NEVER ANSWERS ARE AREAS YOU CAN WORK TO IMPROVE ON!

Bulletin Board Ideas

SPORTSMANSHIP SUPER BOWL

MATERIALS:

Football player cutout, 5 footballs, field goal, border and fabric or paper to cover bulletin board

INSTRUCTIONS:

⊛ In Cut Out Letters-"Kick for the Goal"

⊛ Have a goal post cut out of construction paper on which you have written Good Sportsmanship across the center post

⊛ Have a football player posed as if he has just kicked the football for a field goal. You could enlarge a football player on an over-head projector and then cut it out.

⊛ Have five footballs cut out and have good sportsmanship behaviors written on them. You will attach the footballs to the bulletin board so they look like they are floating through the air towards the goal. Attach them sequentially. Place dash marks between footballs to indicate motion.

> *Respect the Game*
> *Work as a team*
> *Encourage others*
> *Respect others efforts*
> *Win or lose with grace*

MARCH MADNESS NCAA PLAYOFFS

MATERIALS:

Hands/arms cutouts, basketball cutout, paper basketball hoop and net (or a real one if you have access to one), fabric or paper to cover the bulletin board and a border.

⊛ Cut out letters that say "Shoot for Excellence"

⊛ Two arms with hands posed as if they were shooting a ball

⊛ A basketball hoop that you have fashioned out of construction paper or a real net if you have access to one. You can make a paper net by cutting slits in a piece of paper that you have folded to create the three dimensional effect for your hoop.

⊛ Basketball cut out on which you have written Good Sportsmanship. Attach the basketball a little over the center of the bulletin board at the top like it is heading for the hoop. Draw two lines from the hand toward the ball to indicate motion and a dash from the ball to the hoop.

THE OLYMPICS GAMES— WE GO FOR THE GOLD. WE PRACTICE SPORTSMANSHIP!

MATERIALS:

fabric or paper to cover the board, coordinating border. Cutout letters for heading, Olympic rings either made from paper or purchased from a supply company.

INSTRUCTIONS:

- Cover board with paper or fabric and attach border

- **Heading:** We Go For the Gold. We Practice Sportsmanship!

- Attach Olympic Rings

SPORTSMANSHIP WORLD SERIES

MATERIALS:

Baseball player cutout, three bases, pitcher's mound and home plate, border and fabric or paper to cover bulletin board

INSTRUCTIONS:

- In cut out letters-"Hit a Home Run!"

- Construct a baseball diamond out of construction paper on which you have written Good Sportsmanship, home plate

- Have a baseball player posed as if he has just come up to bat. You could enlarge a baseball player on an overhead projector and then cut him out.

- Have pitcher's mound and bases cut out and have good sportsmanship behaviors written on them. Choose from the behaviors below.

  Respect the Game
  Work as a team
  Encourage others
  Respect others efforts
  Win or lose with grace

SPORTSMANSHIP

There is nothing like winning, but it is important to teach our children to be gracious losers. Children often have a hard time understanding the concepts of competition, winning and losing. This is understandable when you consider that children see all of the attention and rewards thrown toward winners, while losers don't receive the same attention. Rick Sitz, in his article Sportsmanship: encouraging our children to be good sports, states that the message children are learning is that people are valued only if they are winners. If that is the message, then should you not have your child participate in sport? Absolutely not; participation in sports can contribute to the development of social competence and self-esteem. Social competence is the ability to get along with and be accepted by others. Self-esteem is developed from the evaluation of one's ability and the evaluation of the responses received by others. Children keenly observe parents' and coaches' responses to their performances by looking for reaction (often nonverbal) of approval or disapproval of their performance and behavior. Too many parents get wrapped up in vicariously living through the lives of their child. Others often have unrealistic expectations about their child, believing that they may someday be a superstar. The best way that parents can promote good sportsmanship is to model the behavior they wish to see in their child. Try to maintain that attitude that you are playing the sport for fun and encourage supporting other members of the team. When you control emotions in frustrating situations, your child is more likely to do the same. Whether you agree with an official's call or the coach's decision, model respect for authority and avoid ridicule and sarcasm. This can sometimes be difficult to achieve when we see professional athletes fighting with each other, fans booing players at professional games and parents at little league games criticizing other players. Many positive experiences can be learned from sports; these concepts can be applied in other areas of life.

- ♛ Taking Turns

- ♛ Sharing playing time

- ♛ Valuing rules

- ♛ Learning to monitor and regulate one's emotions

- ♛ Following directions

- ♛ Cooperating with others

Sportsmanship can be practiced both inside and outside of the classroom.

Scrambled Words

Name: _____ Class: _____ Date: _____

EACH LINE HAS ONE WORD THAT IS SCRAMBLED. UNSCRAMBLE THAT WORD.

1. _ _ _ _ _ _ _ _   haebirov

2. _ _ _ _   lseo

3. _ _ _   jbo

4. _ _ _ _ _ _ _ _   taokrwme

5. _ _ _ _ _ _ _   tecespr

6. _ _ _ _ _ _ _ _ _   orueaecng

7. _ _ _ _ _ _ _ _ _ _ _   egcarolttnau

8. _ _ _ _ _ _ _ _   tspjeroc

9. _ _ _ _ _   sameg

10. _ _ _ _ _ _ _ _ _   engltsini

11. _ _ _ _ _ _ _ _   nefiassr

12. _ _ _ _ _ _ _ _ _ _ _ _ _ _   tslienbipisyro

13. _ _ _   inw

SELECT YOUR ANSWERS FROM THE FOLLOWING WORDS.
ANSWERS CAN BE FOUND ON PAGE 136.

responsibility	projects	behavior	job
games	teamwork	respect	encourage
fairness	win	congratulate	lose
listening			

Secret Code

DECODE THE WORD IN EACH LINE.

1. _ _ _ _ _ dmjfp

2. _ _ _ _ _ _ _ _ xfmjygai

3. _ _ _ sgo

4. _ _ _ _ _ _ _ _ _ fnegramdf

5. _ _ _ _ _ _ _ _ _ _ _ _ egndamxrcmxf

6. _ _ _ _ _ _ _ afpqfex

7. _ _ _ _ _ _ _ _ _ cwpxfnwnd

8. _ _ _ _ _ _ _ _ qagsfexp

9. _ _ _ _ cgpf

10. _ _ _ _ _ _ _ _ oftmkwga

11. _ _ _ ywn

12. _ _ _ _ _ _ _ _ _ _ _ _ _ _ afpqgnpwowcwxh

13. _ _ _ _ _ _ _ _ lmwanfpp

SECRET CODE:

a	b	c	d	e	f	g	h	i	j	k	l	m	n	o	p	q	r	s	t	u	v	w	x	y	z
r	z	l	g	c	e	o	y	k	m	v	f	a	n	b	s	p	u	j	h	d	x	i	t	w	q

SELECT YOUR ANSWERS FROM THE FOLLOWING WORDS.
ANSWERS CAN BE FOUND ON PAGE 136.

encourage	responsibility	games	behavior
respect	win	fairness	listening
congratulate	job	teamwork	projects
lose			

Name: _____ Class: _____ Date: _____

TRY TO FIND THE HIDDEN WORDS.

```
T N D Y R L I S T E N I N G V H N Q
J P C V B N R N I A C J L W X A G O
O R E R W B S A A H B L Z L T G D R
B O Q E N C O U R A G E I I W P V B
D J C S N C V X O F B T U A F V Z R
Z E O P M U T I O W I N N U A O S R
J C N O K L F B Q R V Z P O I B T N
Y T G N V U F E Z E X W E P R E Y P
W S R S G Z M H Z S K Y U B N E E I
W P A I L E C A T P B Y A Y E Z M I
P M T B M T W V E E E C H U S T U L
A D U I M A A I A C G A M E S Q Q C
E B L L D Q R O M T I S O P T P T K
A G A I U B H R W W Z G H O M S G K
U C T T X R P L O S E M O V O Z J T
C P E Y L E Z G R V R R Z G T B T B
W X J P H B H S K V P K V Q L Q V D
U I M E Z Z Q O R K K W X T B T A K
```

SELECT FROM THE FOLLOWING WORDS.
ANSWERS CAN BE FOUND ON PAGE 136.

games	win	listening	lose
fairness	encourage	behavior	congratulate
job	responsibility	projects	teamwork
respect			

Answers

Scrambled Words page 133

1. behavior
2. lose
3. job
4. teamwork
5. respect
6. encourage
7. congratulate
8. projects
9. games
10. listening
11. fairness
12. responsibility
13. win

Secret Code page 134

1. games
2. teamwork
3. job
4. encourage
5. congratulate
6. respect
7. listening
8. projects
9. lose
10. behavior
11. win
12. responsibility
13. fairness

Word Search page 135

```
•  •  •  •  •  L  I  S  T  E  N  I  N  G  •  •  •  •
J  P  •  •  •  •  •  •  •  •  •  •  •  •  •  •  •  •
O  R  •  R  •  •  •  •  •  •  •  •  •  •  •  •  •  •
B  O  •  E  N  C  O  U  R  A  G  E  •  •  •  •  •  •
•  J  C  S  •  •  •  •  •  •  •  F  •  •  •  •
•  E  O  P  •  •  •  •  W  I  N  •  •  A  •  •  •
•  C  N  O  •  •  •  B  R  •  •  •  I  •  •  •
•  T  G  N  •  •  •  E  E  •  •  •  R  •  •  •
•  S  R  S  •  •  •  H  •  S  •  •  •  N  •  •  •
•  •  A  I  •  •  •  A  T  P  •  •  •  E  •  •  •
•  •  T  B  •  •  •  V  E  E  •  •  •  S  •  •  •
•  •  U  I  •  •  •  I  A  C  G  A  M  E  S  •  •
•  •  L  L  •  •  •  O  M  T  •  •  •  •  •  •
•  •  A  I  •  •  •  R  W  •  •  •  •  •  •  •
•  •  T  T  •  •  •  L  O  S  E  •  •  •  •  •  •
•  •  E  Y  •  •  •  •  R  •  •  •  •  •  •  •  •
•  •  •  •  •  •  •  K  •  •  •  •  •  •  •  •  •
•  •  •  •  •  •  •  •  •  •  •  •  •  •  •  •  •
```

Black History Month

COURAGE

Black History Month

The beginning of February signifies the start of Black History Month, a celebration that has existed since 1926. Dr. Carter Woodson organized the first annual Negro History Week, which took place during the second week of February in 1926. Dr. Woodson chose this date because it was close to the birthdays of two men who had a great impact on the lives of blacks in America. These people were Frederick Douglas and Abraham Lincoln. Over time what started out as a celebration that lasted only one week has grown into a month long celebration known as Black History Month.

Black History Month cannot properly be celebrated unless students understand the journey out of slavery into freedom. Therefore, Black History Month the lesson is on The Underground Railroad. The lesson will focus on the character principle of courage. The children's book written by Bernard Waber, *Courage*, is an excellent way to introduce this concept to your students. Courage is what the conductors, station masters and slaves on The Underground Railroad had. And courage is what many famous black Americans had, as they achieved what no other black American had before.

BACKGROUND INFORMATION: SLAVERY AND THE UNDERGROUND RAILROAD

The beginning of the African slave trade can be traced to 1518 when the demand for slaves in the Spanish New World was so great that King Charles I of Spain deemed it necessary to transport slaves directed from Africa to American colonies. From 1530 to the abolition of slavery in 1863-1865 about 10 million Africans were brought by force to the Americas. About 4.5 percent came to North America. The successful use of black African labor on the Brazilian and Caribbean sugar plantations provided a model for European colonists in North America. Most black slaves started arriving in North America in 1619. Before 1860 there were about four million slaves in America. They lived and worked in the South. Most wanted to escape to the North to freedom and thousands of them did. When you were a slave it meant you had nothing you could call your own, not even your name. You, the clothes you wore, the food you ate and the place where you slept all belonged to another person. And your last name was the last name of the person who owned you. Slaves had to do whatever work the owner wanted. Some had to work from sunrise until after dark in the fields. Some slaves worked in the owners' homes. Owners and the overseers could punish you whenever they wanted. Punishment was usually being whipped or other forms of beating. Slaves were often branded just like cattle or other farm animals. You could not walk down a road without a pass from your owners giving you permission to be there. If you didn't have a pass you were beaten or whipped. The worst thing about being a slave was that you could be sold just like a cow, pig, chicken or a piece of furniture. Families were split up and sold to whoever the owner wanted.

Slave markets were humiliating places. When slaves were put up for auction, people would come up to you and open your mouth to look at your teeth, touch and feel your arms and legs to see if they were strong. They would have you bend and twist to see if there was anything wrong with you. The National Underground Railroad Freedom Center in Cincinnati, Ohio has a display of a letter from a John W. Anderson to Thomas Marshall of Natchez, Mississippi dated November 24, 1832. The letter states that:

- Adult males were sold for $550.00 to $650.00

- Females were sold for $400.00 to $425.00 (field workers)

- Men were bought for (17-25 years of age) $400.00-$450.00

- Young boys were bought for $250.00-$350.00

- Girls were bought for (age 15-20 years) $300.00-$325.00

- He bought 16 slaves at a cost of $5955.00 and sold 13 at a cost of $7640.00

And most slaves didn't know how to read or write. In many southern states, whites who taught blacks to read and write could be arrested and fined. Blacks who knew how to read or write and were caught teaching other blacks were beaten, whipped and put in jail.

From the beginning of slavery in America, slaves fled from their owners. These slaves were called fugitives. The majority of these fugitives traveled on the most famous road of all, the Underground Railroad. This really wasn't a real railroad at all. It was a network of secret ways to get out of the South and away from slavery. The Underground Railroad got its name in the year 1831 when a slave by the name of Tice Davids escaped his owner by swimming across the Ohio River to the town of Ripley, Ohio. The slave owner could see Davids in front of him crossing the river but when he got to shore he vanished from sight. The owner searched the riverbank, the town and the surrounding area, but there was no sign of the slave. The confused owner gave up the search; he shook his head and said, "He must have gone on an underground road!" Steam engines had just been invented, and people who knew the story began saying that Davids had escaped on the underground railroad.

Underground was a perfect name for the system because it was secret, and you couldn't see it, and because, it appeared that it ran regularly and smoothly. Most of the time you walked on the Underground Railroad and the journey could take two months. Only sometimes would you ride on a real railroad, a horse drawn carriage, a horse or a boat. As you traveled you stayed in secret locations, hiding places called stations or station houses. People who helped the runaway slaves were called railroad workers, and the people who would lead you to the next station were called conductors. Station masters were the people who would feed you and give you a place to sleep until you left for the next station. Sometimes you had to hide in forests, swamps, caves and big trees. You might have to climb a tree, and sleep there during the day and travel by night. While traveling you ate what you could find like nuts, roots, berries, corn, or apples. You might be lucky and catch a fish or rabbit, but most of the time you were too afraid to build a fire and cook because someone might see the smoke. You faced many dangers while trying to escape, but the biggest danger was being caught. While hiding in the swamp or forest, you had to worry about wild animals, alligators, bears or poisonous snakes. Sometimes station masters hid you in houses or barns behind walls, under the floor or in pieces of furniture.

Many type of people worked on the Underground Railroad. Blacks and whites, adults and children, men and women, all of these people were united in their belief that slavery was wrong. There were both Northerners and some Southerners who helped the runaway slaves. But most of the people who helped were ordinary people who made an extraordinary difference. A few of the conductors and station masters became famous like Harriet Tubman. She was such a successful conductor that a reward of $40,000 was offered for her capture. Famous station masters were Levi Coffin and Thomas Garrett both Quakers. Quakers were a religious group whose beliefs taught them that all people were equal and there should be no such thing as a slave and a master. A person aiding fugitives to escape was in danger of being jailed, fined or having their home or property damaged.

The safest places in the country to go to were northern states. By 1800 slavery had ended in most of these states. Many slaves fled to Cincinnati, Philadelphia, New York, and Boston. But in 1850 a new law made it unsafe even in northern states. This law said that slave hunters could come into a northern state, find you and take you back to the South. So you had to journey even farther north to Canada. The minute you set foot in Canada you were 100% free.

In 1860 South Carolina seceded in December and more states followed in the next year. The Civil War began in 1861 and lasted four years until 1865. During this vicious conflict 623,000 lives were lost. In 1863 on January 1st, President Abraham Lincoln decreed that all slaves in Rebel territory were free. In 1865 with the 13th amendment to the United States Constitution slavery was outlawed.

Quilts and the Underground Railroad

In the book *Hidden in Plain View*, by Jacqueline Tobin and Raymond Dobard, Ph.D, they talk about how certain quilt blocks were possibly used as a code to guide slaves to freedom. In 1994 Jacqueline Tobin met a woman named Ozella McDaniel Williams from South Carolina. She shared that quilts were used to communicate information about the Underground Railroad. Ms. Williams and her family's oral history there were ten quilts used to direct the slaves to get ready to run to freedom. In the book *The Secret to Freedom* by Marcia Vaughn states that quilts were used to communicate information to aid escaping slaves.

Messages contained in common quilt patterns could transmit information to slaves to assist them in their journey North. Quilt patterns were assigned signs, symbols and codes. Messages contained in the quilts displayed could tell the slaves to:

> Pack their tools, supplies, belongings and clothes they would need when they escaped.

> Tell them when it was time to run and escape on the Underground Railroad.

> Let the slaves know what path to follow on their escape route. Should they travel through the mountains and avoid the main roads, or should they journey to Cleveland, Ohio and use the major crossroads into Canada?

BLACK HISTORY MONTH

COURAGE AND THE UNDERGROUND RAILROAD

OBJECTIVES:

🌿 Students will understand the character concept of courage as it relates to themselves and the Underground Railroad.

🌿 Students will be able to explain three concepts relating to the Underground Railroad.

MATERIALS NEEDED:

A Quilt for students to sit on, materials for slave auction, quilt (poster boards) for board and cards for review activity, masking tape, container for students to pull the cards out of and a book to read to the class about the Underground Railroad.

APPLAUSE FOR THIS LESSON:

Awesome Applause- Raise hands over heads, clap one time, bend at waist and bow down towards the floor and say "Awwwwesome." Because having courage is "awesome!"

1. Introduce the lesson by sharing that today we are starting a two part lesson for Black History Month, which is the month of February. During this month we are going to learn about the character concept of courage. We will learn about the Underground Railroad and famous black Americans who showed courage.

2. Start by asking the students, "What is courage?" You could record their answers on an overhead or write them on the board. Then write: Courage is overcoming your fear. Being brave enough to do what you should do even when you are scared. There are two types of courage.

   🌿 "Amazing Courage"- Olympic athletes, soldiers, firefighters, doctors, paramedics, police and people who help others in dangerous situations.

   🌿 "Day by Day Courage"- Giving a report in front of your class, not being jealous when someone gets more attention than you, playing a musical instrument in a recital, not telling secrets, starting over on a paper or project when you do it wrong and admitting when you make a mistake.

   🌿 Then ask your students, how have we seen courage in each other?

   If you have the book by Bernard Waber, Courage, you could share some of his examples of courage. He defines courage as being in two categories. He even gives examples of pets having courage.

3. Spread the quilt on the floor and have students come up and sit on it. Share the story of the Underground Railroad. Use the information that you feel is appropriate to the grade level you are teaching. Ask how these people showed courage. Was it "Day by Day Courage" or "Amazing Courage?" Or was it both?

4. Read a story to the class about the Underground Railroad.

5. Use the cards to review the story and have students place the cards on the poster board quilt on the board in the blank spaces. Be sure to have their fellow students reward their answers with awesome applause. Conclude the lesson by asking the students, "What have we learned about courage?"

6. Leave a follow up activity with the teacher to use with the class, either a work sheet or a quilt block to be put together to form their class's "Freedom Quilt."

BOOKS ABOUT THE UNDERGROUND RAILROAD:

A Good Night For Freedom—Barbara Oleyik Morrow, author's notes include additional information about Levi Coffin considered by many to be the President of the Underground Railroad.

Sweet Clara and the Freedom Quilt—Deborah Hopkinson

Almost to Freedom—Vaunda Micheaux Nelson

Barefoot Escape on the Underground Railroad—Pamela Duncan Edwards

Allen Jay and the Underground Railroad—Marlene Targ Brill

The Patchwork Path A Quilt Map to Freedom—Bettye Stroud

The Secret to Freedom—Marcia Vaughan

Aunt Harriet's Underground Railroad in the Sky—Faith Ringgold

If You Traveled on The Underground Railroad—Ellen Levine

Show Way—Jacqueline Woodson. The story of a slave family and their ancestors and how quilts showed the way. Newberry Honor Book

The Legend of Freedom Hill—Linda James Altman

* MultiCultural Theme

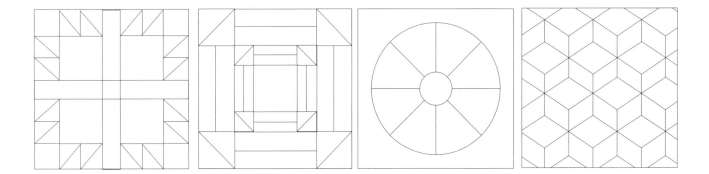

1. Select a quilt pattern from this lesson. Have each student color one block and cut it out. Then attach each student's quilt block to a large piece of colored paper such as those that would be used to cover a bulletin board. Display in the hallway or classroom bulletin board for black history month with an explanation of the clue it gave slaves on the Underground Railroad.

2. Make your own quilt block. Divide a square into four equal pieces. On one of these four blocks have the students draw their school and then in the three remaining blocks have them draw three locations around their school. The dividing lines of the quilt blocks may be streets around your school. Or you could give each of the students a different prominent landmark in your community and have them draw it in one block and in the three remaining blocks have them draw three locations around this prominent landmark. The dividing lines would be the streets around the landmark. Place all the students' blocks together, and you will have a map like Clara did in *Sweet Clara and the Freedom Quilt* by Deborah Hopkinson. Attach each student's quilt block to a large piece of colored paper like those used to cover a bulletin board. Display in the hallway or classroom bulletin board.

Activity: Lesson Preparation

DIRECTIONS FOR MAKING QUILT FOR BOARD

MATERIALS NEEDED:

You will need four pieces of poster board all the same color. Construction paper for boarder, 8 cutout designs (Ellison Die cuts are fine) scissors, glue, and masking tape. Make four cutouts of one color design such as a sun and four of another like a heart.

DIRECTIONS:

- Trim each piece of poster board to measure 22 inches by 15 inches

- Lay the poster boards together with edges touching to form the shape of a quilt.

- Cut construction paper strips to form a border 2 1/2 inches wide. Glue this boarder to two side edges of your poster board.

- Cut construction paper strips in one inch wide lengths and place on the boards. You will be dividing the boards into quilt blocks 5 1/2 inches by 9 1/4 inches. Glue the strips to the boards.

- Place your cutout designs in the quilt blocks. Using same design in the upper left corner quilt block of each board, and the other design you selected in the lower right corner quilt block of each board.

- Laminate all four boards. They can be easily transported from room to room and stored. You may attach the boards to a dry erase board or blackboard with masking tape.

In the blank square of the quilt, students will be placing blocks of construction paper 4 1/4 inches by 4 inches. On these blocks you have the following words on each card; you may print the words both on the front and back. Laminate these cards so you may use them again. When the student draws the block out of the container for the activity, he may choose which word he wants to relate to your lesson. This is a fun way to review your lesson and the story you read of the Underground Railroad. Attach these blocks with masking tape. Suggested words you can choose from:

Slave

Master

Station House

Conductor

Courage

Kindness

Caring

Trustworthy

Respect

Civil War

Citizenship

Canada

Quilts

Plantation

Overseer

Activity: Slave Auction

1. MAKE THREE SIGNS: One sign says *girl for sale*, one sign says *boy for sale* and the third says *teacher (or woman/man) for sale*. You may decorate these signs with coin or money stickers. Laminate. Punch holes in each sign and tie a string of yarn to each so the sign may be placed around a person's neck.

2. You will be the auctioneer and sell the classroom teacher and one male and female student to the highest bidder following the price guidelines stated in the background of the lesson.

3. REFLECTION: Ask students what feelings these people had who were being sold. What if it were a mother/father and their children? How would they feel?

OPTIONAL MATERIALS:

A black top hat for you as the auctioneer and play money for the students to bid with.

OPTIONAL KINDERGARTEN ACTIVITY:

Select one boy and two girls to be the students who purchase the other students and teacher who are for sale. Have the boy wear a top hat, the girls a shawl around their shoulders and white gloves. Give these students play money. Have the class bid on how much each dressed up student will pay for the teacher and students.

The Bear's Paw

The Bear's Paw pattern instructed runaways to follow the bear tracks through the mountains, staying away from the roads.

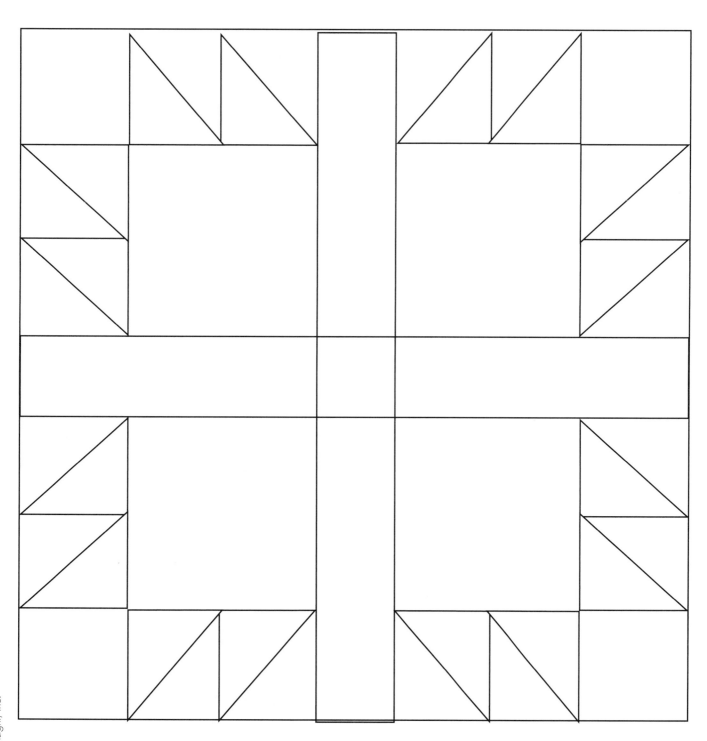

The Monkey Wrench

The Monkey Wrench alerted slaves to pack
their belongings and provisions to help them
survive their journey.

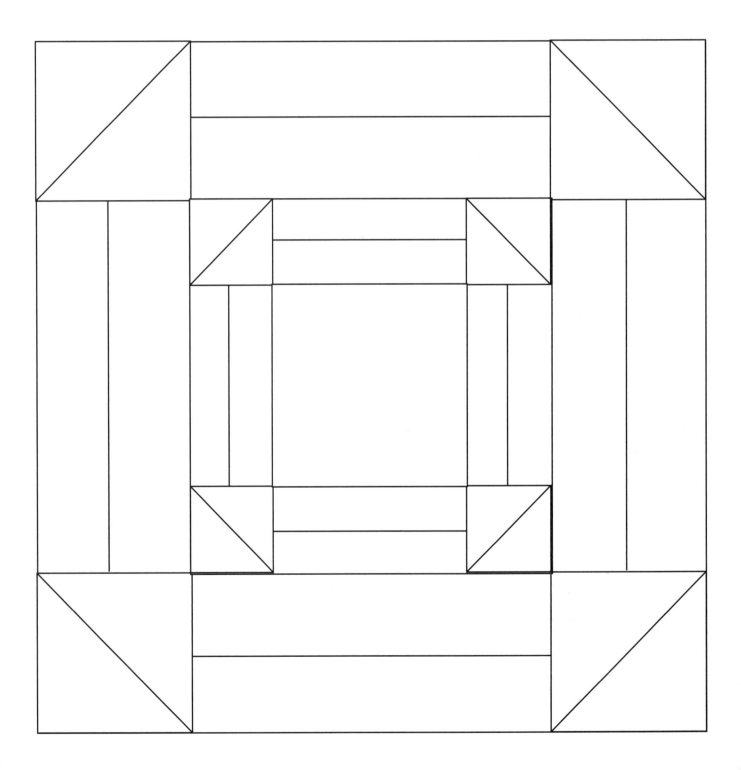

The Tumbling Blocks

The Tumbling Blocks pattern announced
that it was time to escape.

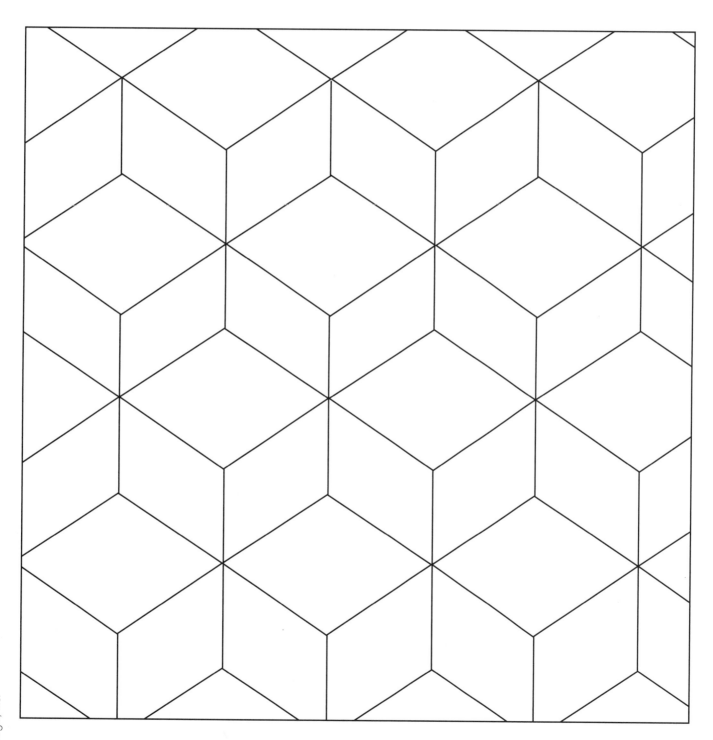

The Wagon Wheel

The Wagon Wheel pattern told slaves to
pack their belongings and provisions to help
them survive their journey.

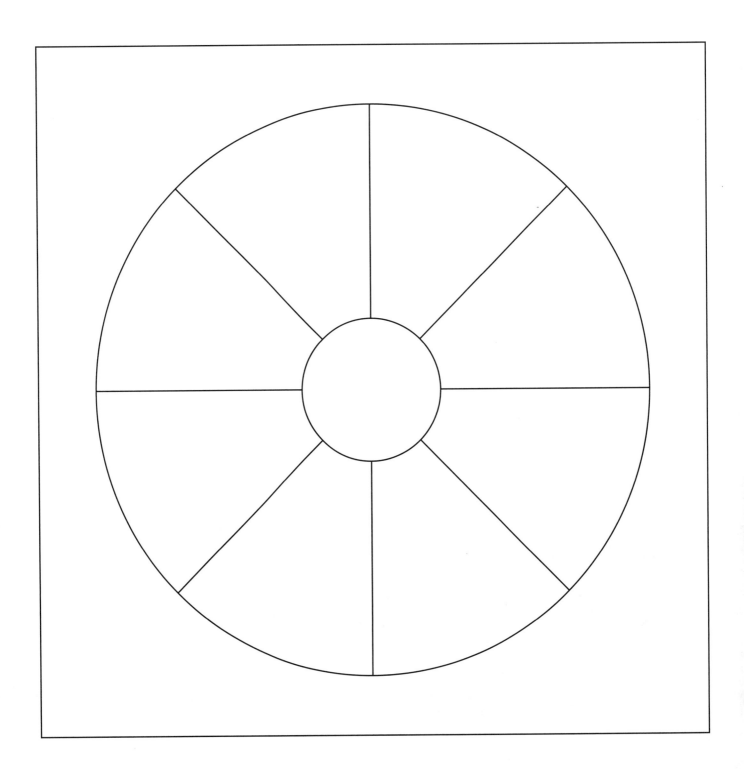

A Green Light for Courage

COLOR THE CIRCLE GREEN IF THIS SHOWS COURAGE.
COLOR THE CIRCLE RED IF THIS DOES NOT SHOW COURAGE.

O Courage is riding your bicycle without
   training wheels for the first time.

O Courage is not making up after an argument with a friend.

O Courage is keeping the juicy secret you promised not to tell.

O Courage is the bottom of the ninth, the score is tied,
   your team has two outs and you are up to bat.

O Courage is telling your mom you really don't know
   how your pants got ripped, when you really do.

O Courage is starting over when you make a mistake.

O Courage is letting people pick on your little sister.

O Courage is walking away from a fight.

O Courage is ignoring someone's mean words.

O Courage is doing the right thing even when
   it is the hard thing to do.

BLACK HISTORY MONTH

The beginning of February signifies the start of Black History Month, a celebration that has existed since 1926. Dr. Carter Woodson organized the first annual Negro History Week which took place during the second week of February in 1926. Dr. Woodson chose this date because it was close to the birthdays of two men who had a great impact on the lives of blacks in America. These people were Frederick Douglas and Abraham Lincoln. Over time what started out as a celebration that lasted only one week has grown into a month-long celebration known as Black History Month.

How can Black History Month be celebrated by the family? Many communities offer cultural events that honor the contribution of famous black Americans. Museums, art galleries, symphony orchestras and community choruses often feature special programs during this month to help celebrate the contributions made by African Americans to the arts. Visit your local library and get books to read as a family to learn more about the significant contributions of black Americans. A good place to start teaching children about the significance of Black History Month is to start at the beginning, with the story of slavery. Many wonderful books have been written about the Underground Railroad that are easy to read and educational as well. During this month long celebration it is good to talk with your children about the character concept of courage. Courage is what was shown by the slaves who escaped from the south. And courage is what the station masters and conductors who helped slaves escape on the Underground Railroad had. The biography section of the library is a wonderful section to check out with your children to learn more about the contributions of George Washington Carver, Harriet Tubman, Jesse Owens, Jackie Robinson, Sojourner Truth, Booker T. Washington and Rosa Parks. All of these people were amazing in their accomplishments and achievements.

" Each time a man stands up for an ideal,
or acts to improve the lot of others
or strikes out against injustice,
he send forth a tiny ripple of hope,
building a current that can sweep down the mightiest
walls of oppression and resistance."

—Robert F. Kennedy

Chapter Nine

Groundhog Day
PREDICTION AND GOAL SETTING

Prediction and Goal Setting

According to an old belief in the United States and Canada, February 2 was supposed to be a good day to look for signs of spring. In these countries the emergence of a groundhog from its burrow is said to foretell the weather for the next six weeks. The beginning of the month of February falls roughly halfway between the winter solstice and spring equinox. Among the Celts it was a time of anticipation of the birth of farm animals and the planting of crops. During the Middle Ages there was a belief that the badger and the bear interrupted their hibernation to appear on this day. This is the day on which English farmers waited for a hedgehog or bear to peek out of its burrow after a long winter sleep. German farmers watched for a badger. If the day was sunny, the animal saw its shadow. Folks thought that the animal must be afraid of its shadow and would run back into its burrow. There the animal would sleep for six

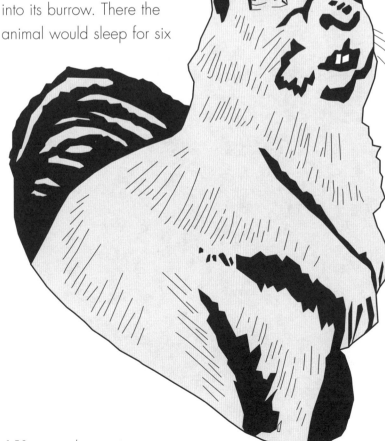

more weeks, and spring would be late that year. German and English settlers in North America switched the animal in the legend to a groundhog; because that's the animal they saw more often. And the groundhog has been our unofficial "spring forecaster" ever since.

Since 1887 an animal in Punxsutawney, Pennsylvania has been center stage of a media event. His name is Punxsutawney Phil; weathermen and newspaper photographers all want his picture. Records say that Phil's prediction has a correlation of less than 40 percent accuracy. Science says that whether or not the groundhog emerges is related to how much fat it was able to store before going into hibernation. Local Pennsylvania supporters have designed a festival in February around Phil's tradition. Canada has a number of groundhogs that serve as local weather predictors; the best known is Wiarton Willie.

Whether you are trying to predict the weather by a groundhog's shadow or avoiding cracks in the sidewalk because you might break your mother's back, these are interesting superstitions but if you want something to happen, you need to plan for it and set goals. The lesson for this holiday is prediction and goal setting.

LESSON—PREDICTION / GOAL SETTING

OBJECTIVES:

At the end of the lesson the children will be able to explain the belief surrounding Groundhog Day.

At the end of the lesson the children will be able to list how to work towards a goal.

At the end of the lesson the children will be able explain why superstitions do not predict success.

MATERIALS:

Overhead projector, overheads, story to share, activity sheet for opening lesson, worksheet and song lyrics, one for each student if you are using them.

APPLAUSE-"ROUND OF APPLAUSE"

Clap hands in a round circular motion. Why round of applause? Because that is what you deserve for setting goals.

1. Open the lesson with the background of the tradition of Groundhog Day. Then use the activity using superstitions to open the lesson. Reward students for their discussion and participation with "Round of Applause."

2. Using the overheads in the following order, teach the lesson that prediction is much more reliable when you set goals you are working towards.

   - Common superstitions—ask questions and generate a discussion why these are not really true.

   - Prediction and Goal Setting

   - Ideas—then use work sheet for lesson and share the story you have selected. After story, discuss how it relates to setting goals or the Groundhog Day tradition.

3. End the lesson with teaching and singing the song, and then remind students how important it is to set goals. Leave the class with follow-up activity.

Books

GROUNDHOG DAY

Punxsutawney Phyllis—Susanna Leonard Hill

Groundhog Day—Michelle Aki Becker

Fluffy Meets the Groundhog—Kate McMullan

Geoffrey Groundhog Predicts the Weather—Bruce Koscielniak

Go to Sleep Groundhog—Judy Cox

Gregory's Shadow—Don Freeman

It's Groundhog Day—Steve Kroll

Gretchen Groundhog, It's Your Day!—Abby Levine

SETTING GOALS

Eddy's Dream—Miriam Cohen

The Fish Who Could Wish—John Bush & Korky Paul

Marta and the Bicycle—Germano Zullo

The Sign Painter—Allen Say

Common Superstitions

GROUNDHOGS WHO SEE THEIR
SHADOW CAN PREDICT THE WEATHER.

FRIDAY THE THIRTEENTH IS AN UNLUCKY DAY.

A RABBIT'S FOOT BRINGS GOOD LUCK.

AN APPLE A DAY KEEPS THE DOCTOR AWAY.

STEP ON A CRACK, YOU BREAK
YOUR MOTHER'S BACK.

A CRICKET IN THE HOUSE BRINGS GOOD LUCK.

AN ITCHY PALM MEANS MONEY
WILL COME YOUR WAY.

IF YOU WALK UNDER A LADDER
YOU WILL HAVE BAD LUCK.

Prediction and Goal Setting

The best way to predict your future is to create it.

Decide on what you would like to improve. What you want to improve is your goal.

Create an action plan to work on what you want to improve. Break it down into steps of what to work on to achieve the goal.

Don't get discouraged— keep working on what you want to improve. Goals worth accomplishing take time.

BEING A BETTER STUDENT:

Don't bring a rabbit's foot for good luck!

INSTEAD:

Improve listening skills.

Follow instructions.

Create a homework schedule.

Get homework done on time.

RESULTS:

Improved grades.

Improved test scores.

BEING A BETTER FRIEND:

"If you blow out all the candles on your birthday cake with the first breath, you will get whatever you wish for."

Instead:

Caring ....use no mean words
Trustworthy ....I do what I say I will do
Fair ....in actions, words & deeds
Honest ....with myself and others
Dependable ....you can count on me
Patient ....with myself and others
Considerate ....think of others first
Loyal ....faithful to self and others
Forgiving ....no paybacks
Responsible ....for everything I say and do
Respectful ....of others and myself

Results:

More Friends.
Better relationships with people in my life.

BEING A BETTER FAMILY MEMBER:

"Crossing your fingers helps to avoid bad luck and helps your wish come true."

Instead:

Pitch in and HELP out.

LISTEN with your heart and your head.

RESPONSIBLE—actions, words and deeds.

DO what I am supposed to do, WHEN I am supposed to do it, WITHOUT BEING ASKED.

PATIENT—with family members and self.

NO BAD ATTITUDES.

Loyal—my FAMILY is a priority.

CLEAN your room.

PICK UP after yourself. If you mess it up, clean it up.

SUPPORT other family members when they need it.

Results:

Better family relationships.
You earn more respect.

Opening Lesson Activity

INSTRUCTIONS:

Have students see if they can complete the common superstitions listed below.
Then discuss whether these are superstitions or factual predictions?

COMMON SUPERSTITIONS:

✳ Groundhogs that see their shadow..........................can predict the weather.

✳ Friday the thirteenth...is an unlucky day.

✳ A rabbit's foot brings...good luck.

✳ An apple a day ....keeps the doctor away.

✳ Step on a crack ....you break your mother's back.

✳ A cricket in the house ....brings good luck.

✳ An itchy palm means..money will come your way.

✳ If you walk under a ladder ....you will have bad luck.

✳ If you break a mirror ....you will have seven years bad luck.

✳ To open an umbrella in the house ....is to bring bad luck.

✳ A cat has ....nine lives.

✳ Cold hand ....warm heart.

✳ To drop silverware means ....company is coming.

Goal Setting

INSTEAD OF:

"A beginner will always have good luck: beginner's luck."

Make a plan to reach your goal.
The best way to predict your future is to create it.

I would like to improve at _____

_____.

My goal is to _____

_____.

Four steps I need to take in order to reach my goal are:

1._____

_____.

2._____

_____.

3._____

_____.

4._____

_____.

MY ACTION PLAN:

List the actions you need to take for each step to reach my goal.

Step 1._____

_____.

completion date_____

Step 2._____

_____.

completion date_____

Step 3._____

_____.

completion date_____

Step 4._____

_____.

completion date_____

Goal Setting

**INSTEAD OF "LOOKING FOR THE POT OF GOLD AT THE END OF THE RAINBOW,"
ACHIEVE YOUR OWN POT OF GOLD BY WORKING TOWARDS REACHING YOUR GOAL.**

The best things about reaching my goal will be_____

_____

I will have to give up these things to reach my goal _____

_____

Working towards my goals will affect these areas of my life; explain how it will affect on the blank space and circle if it will be positive or negative.

1. Friends _____(POSITIVE/NEGATIVE)

2. Family _____(POSITIVE/NEGATIVE)

3. School _____(POSITIVE/NEGATIVE)

SONG: I'm Working on Improving Me

SUNG TO THE TUNE OF

I'M PICKING UP A BABY BUMBLE BEE

I'm working on some goals to make me better.
I'm making plans and sticking to them too.
I'm making choices and improving my grades.
Why don't you come and try it out too!

I'm working on some goals to make me better.
I'm not counting on rabbits' feet or clovers.
I'm making choices based on what I want.
Why don't you come and try it out too!

I'm working on some goals to make me better.
I'm helping myself be the best that I can be.
I'm making choices and helping myself.
Why don't you start working on goals too!

Bulletin Board

"REACH FOR THE STARS, SET GOALS"

MATERIALS NEEDED:
fabric or paper to cover board, matching border, one large star cut out, letters for heading, yarn or string, phrases typed in large font on your computer.

INSTRUCTIONS:
- Cover bulletin board with paper or fabric, attach border.

- Attach heading letters and place star in top right side of board. Attach phrase to star that says "My goal is....."

- Attach phrases of goal setting on computer at different levels and attach string yarn to each and attach the string or yarn to the star.

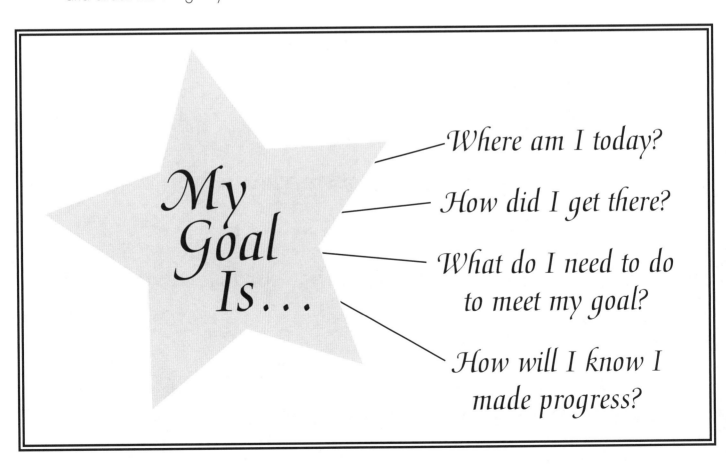

Craft: Shadow Art

TALK WITH CHILDREN ABOUT GROUNDHOG DAY AND SHADOWS.

MATERIALS:

flashlights, masking tape, white chalk, marker pencil and black construction paper

INSTRUCTIONS

- ✍ Tape black paper onto the wall and have students hold their hands* in front of it while shining the flashlight to create a shadow print.

- ✍ Trace their outline shadows.

- ✍ Have students cut out tracing.

- ✍ Using the white chalk, pencil or marker have students make a list of what goal or goals they have decided to work towards.

VARIATION:

trace their silhouette.

GROUNDHOG DAY

According to an old belief in the United States and Canada, February 2 was supposed to be a good day to look for signs of spring. In these countries the emergence of a groundhog from its burrow is said to foretell the weather for the next six weeks. The beginning of the month of February falls roughly halfway between the winter solstice and spring equinox. Among the Celts it was a time of anticipation of the birth of farm animals and the planting of crops. During the Middle Ages there was a belief that the badger and the bear interrupted their hibernation to appear on this day. This is the day on which English farmers waited for a hedgehog or bear to peek out of its burrow after a long winter sleep. German farmers watched for a badger. If the day was sunny, the animal saw its shadow. Folks thought that the animal must be afraid of its shadow and would run back into its burrow. There the animal would sleep for six more weeks and spring would be late that year. German and English settlers in North America switched the animal in the legend to a groundhog, because that's the animal they saw more often. And the groundhog has been our unofficial "spring forecaster" ever since.

Since 1887 an animal in Punxsutawney, Pennsylvania has been center stage of a media event. His name is Punxsutawney Phil, weathermen and newspaper photographers all want his picture. Records say that Phil's prediction has a correlation of less than 40 percent accuracy. Science says that whether or not the groundhog emerges is related to how much fat it was able to store before going into hibernation. Local Pennsylvania supporters have designed a festival in February around Phil's tradition. Canada has a number of groundhogs that serve as local weather predictors; the best known is Wiarton Willie.

Whether you are trying to predict the weather by a groundhog's shadow or avoiding cracks in the sidewalk because you might break your mother's back these are interesting superstitions; but if you want something to happen, you need to plan for it and set goals.

Crossword Puzzle

PREDICTION AND GOAL SETTING

Name: _____ Class: _____ Date: _____

FILL IN THE CROSSWORD PUZZLE BY USING THE CLUES.

ACROSS

1. Decide what you would like to _ _ _ _ _ _ _.
2. Break it down into steps of what to work on to _ _ _ _ _ _ _ the goal.
3. Goals help you know where you are _ _ _ _ _.
4. Superstitions do not _ _ _ _ _ _ _ the future but they are fun to read.
5. Don't get _ _ _ _ _ _ _ _ _ _ _. Keep working on what you want to improve.
6. An apple a day will not keep the doctor away but will be a _ _ _ _ _ _ _ choice for a snack.

DOWN

1. A rabbit's foot or a four leaf clover do not give you good luck but _ _ _ _ _ _ _ towards a goal will.
2. Goals worth _ _ _ _ _ _ _ _ _ _ _ _ take time.
3. The best way to predict your _ _ _ _ _ _ is to set a goal.
4. Create an action _ _ _ _ to work on what you want to improve.

SELECT YOUR ANSWERS FROM THE FOLLOWING WORDS.
ANSWERS CAN BE FOUND ON PAGE .

improve	healthy	discouraged	working
plan	accomplishing	future	achieve
going	predict		

Scrambled Words

PREDICTION AND GOAL SETTING

Name: _____Class:_____Date: _____

EACH LINE HAS ONE WORD THAT IS SCRAMBLED. UNSCRAMBLE THAT WORD.

1. A rabbit's foot or a four leaf clover do not give you good

   luck but _ _ _ _ _ _ _ towards a goal will.   irgokwn

2. Create an action _ _ _ _ to work on what you want to improve.   anpl

3. Break it down into steps of what to work on to _ _ _ _ _ _ _ the goal. aihvece

4. An apple a day will not keep the doctor away but will be a _ _ _ _ _ _ _ snack. yatelhh

5. The best way to predict your _ _ _ _ _ _ is to set a goal.   rtuuef

6. Superstitions do no _ _ _ _ _ _ _ the future but they are fun to read. detipcr

7. Goals help you know where you are _ _ _ _ _ .   oging

8. Don't get _ _ _ _ _ _ _ _ _ _ _. Keep working on what you want to improve. cdosgeiaudr

9. Goals worth _ _ _ _ _ _ _ _ _ _ _ _ take time.   hoalimcsgicpn

10. Decide what you would like to _ _ _ _ _ _ _.   mpeivor

SELECT YOUR ANSWERS FROM THE FOLLOWING WORDS.
ANSWERS CAN BE FOUND ON PAGE .

going	improve	achieve	discouraged
plan	future	healthy	accomplishing
working	predict		

PREDICTION AND GOAL SETTING

Name: _____ Class: _____ Date: _____

TRY TO FIND THE HIDDEN WORDS.

```
I U Z Z H K O R R W O R K I N G E D
M C B L I V S X G S J F O V B Q Y L
B D F P P A A V A Z X T B W F W D J
M I M P R O V E Z T R A L O J P X X
Y S E V B Z P Z T B V R T P C G Y G
G C I P T A A C H I E V E P N S W G
L O L L R C C V L E U S X Z G U Z Q
I U I A Z E L C C K A A L M U Q R N
V R C N N S D H O D V L K D Z H I O
D A N A G L F I U M D V T U G W R A
G G Q Q M B T U C C P O N H C Y X S
O E K Z K C C L T T T L V M Y I C K
Y D L I I L P S U I Z I K G S L Q
N D R G V Q W K C N R C D S T Z G U
M C C Q F P R O I B A E S J H W K Z
J N X M W P Q H F T R Z L T Q I O U
J T Z X X D Y H A S B S I F F T N G
T E Q H P X D M J W A I F X J W H G
```

SELECT FROM THE FOLLOWING WORDS.
ANSWERS CAN BE FOUND ON PAGE 172.

predict	working	healthy	future
going	achieve	improve	plan
discouraged	accomplishing		

Answers

Scrambled words page 170

1. working
2. plan
3. achieve
4. healthy
5. future
6. predict
7. going
8. discouraged
9. accomplishing
10. improve

Crossword Puzzle page 169

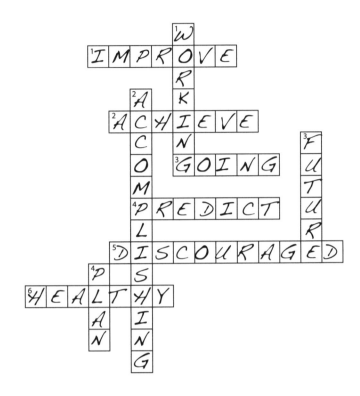

Word Search page 171

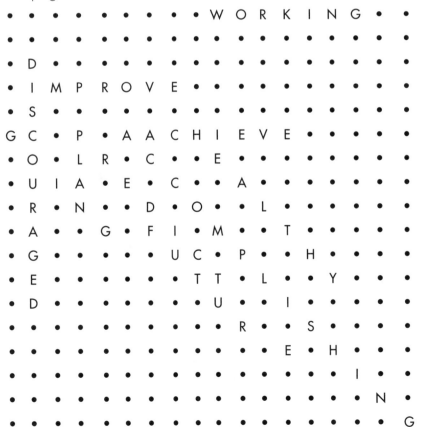

Valentine's Day
KINDNESS

Valentine's Day

KINDNESS

The History of Valentine's Day- Each February around the world, flowers, candy, valentine cards and gifts are exchanged between loved ones. All are given in the name of St. Valentine. This mysterious St. Valentine has many myths and legends about him. The Catholic Church recognizes at least three different saints named Valentine or Valentinus who were martyred. One legend has Valentine being a priest who served in Rome during the third century. The Emperor Claudius II decided that single men made better soldiers than married men. He outlawed marriage for young men. Valentine disagreed with the decision and still performed marriages in secret for young couples. When Claudius found out, he ordered him put to death. Other stories have Valentine attempting to assist Christians in escaping the harsh Roman prisons. One legend has Valentine falling in love himself with a young girl believed to be the jailer's daughter. He met the girl while in prison himself. Before his death he allegedly wrote a love letter to the girl and signed it "From your Valentine," a phrase that is still used today.

Although the truth is hard to tell from these stories, Valentine's appeal is as a sympathetic, heroic and romantic figure. Valentine is still a very popular saint in England and France today.

Valentine greetings were popular as far back as the Middle Ages. Written valentines didn't appear until 1400. Valentine's Day started to be celebrated in Great Britain around the seventeenth century. In the middle of the eighteenth century it was common for all friends and those in love to exchange small gifts of affection and hand written notes. In the end of the eighteen century printed cards started to replace written notes. This was brought about mainly because of the improvement of printing technology. The valentine greeting card made it easier to express emotions and postage rates made it favorable to send valentines. Americans exchanged handmade valentines in the early 1700's until Esther A. Howland began to sell the first mass-produced valentines in America. Her valentines were known as "scrap" because they were made of real lace, ribbons and colorful pictures. The oldest valentine is on display at the British Museum.

Valentine's Day

LESSON—KINDNESS

OBJECTIVES:

- Students will be able to explain three facts about the history of Valentine's Day.

- Students will be able to explain how kindness grows.

- Students will be able to list four ways to practice kindness.

MATERIALS NEEDED:

Valentines to use for grouping students, questions for each group, overheads, kindness pledge, a story

"VALENTINE'S DAY APPLAUSE"

Clap hands in front one time. Right hand over heart patting gently three times. Big smile on face.

1. Open the lesson with the background of Valentine's Day. Adjust the information to the age of your students.

2. Tell the students today we are going to learn about kindness. It is important to be kind and especially at Valentine's Day.

3. Divide the students into groups as listed in the lesson activity. Use Valentines to sort them into groups and assign a question for each group to brainstorm ways to be kind in that situation. Have the group leader selected as the person who has the shortest hair, biggest or smallest foot, etc. Have groups report to class reward groups with "Valentine's Day Applause."

4. Using the overheads in the following order teach the lesson about kindness:

   - Kindness is
   - You can show.....
   - The secret
   - Selfish

5. Read the selected story to the students. Discuss deeds of kindness in the story.

6. Use application activity with students either Thumbs Up/Thumbs Down or Kindness in Practice Reward with Valentine's Day Applause.

7. End lesson with this overhead Kindness Pass It On! And Kindness Pledge. Wish all the students a Happy Valentine's Day and tell them to remember that kindness makes our world a better place.

Books

VALENTINE'S DAY

Somebody Loves You, Mr. Hatch—Eileen Spinelli

Arthur's Valentine—Marc Brown

Roses are Pink, Your Feet Really Stink—Diane deGroat

The Day It Rained Hearts—Felicia Bond

Heart to Heart—George Shannon

I Like You—Sandol Stoddard

Heartprints—P.K. Hallinan

KINDNESS

I Like Your Buttons!—Sarah Marwil Lamstein

Because Brian Hugged His Mother—David L. Rice

Glenna's Seeds—Nancy Edwards

Feathers & Fur—Audrey Penn

Abel and Wolf—Lairla Sergio

How Kind—Mary Murphy

One Smile—Cindy McKinley

Simon Can't Say Hippopotamus—
       Bonnie Highsmith Taylor

A Circle of Friends—Giroa Carmi

The Brand New Kid—Katie Couric

Junie B. Jones and the Mushy Gushy Valentine—
       Barbara Park *

Nate the Great and the Mushy Valentine—
       Marjorie Weinman Sharmat *

                    * *Too long for one class reading*

Kindness Is...

SHOWING THAT YOU CARE ABOUT ALL TYPES OF PEOPLE:

friends and acquaintances

tall people, short people

old people, young people

*handicapped people
and not handicapped people*

popular people and regular people

*people who need help
and people who don't*

SHOWING YOU CARE ABOUT THINGS LIKE:

our world

community

school

classmates

You Can Show Kindness In...

BIG WAYS

or

Small ways!

Kindness makes others feel good. It can also make other people want to be kind as well.

The thing about kindness is, it grows and grows and **grows** some more. *And it eventually comes back to you!*

AVOID THINGS THAT
YOU WOULDN'T WANT
TO HAPPEN TO YOU:

THE SECRET TO PRACTICING KINDNESS IS TO REMEMBER TO TREAT OTHERS LIKE YOU WANT TO BE TREATED.

Gossip

Rumors

Laughing

Teasing

Mean Words

Not Sharing

Excluding people

Making fun of others

Clubs & Cliques

Bullying

Going for payback

"I'm not going to be your friend if…"

SELFISH
IS THE OPPOSITE OF
KINDNESS

People who think only of themselves first.

You have to play what I want to play.

You have to play only with
me or I won't be your friend.

I'm all that... just look at me!

Having to be first all the time.

Having to get the first and
last word in a conversation.

You have to do things my way.

Thinking they never do anything to "bug" others.

Not listening or paying attention when friends talk.

Kindness: Pass It On!

Forgive mistakes • Smile at someone new • Listen with your head and heart • Apologize • Hug someone • Say, "After you" • Smile • Pick up trash • Invite someone to play • Listen to your grandparents stories • Forgive and forget • Thank a teacher • Do chores without being asked • Play with your pet • Make a new friend • Be tolerant of differences • Say, "hello" • Encourage friends • Call a lonely student • Cheer someone up • Read to a younger brother or sister • Help out • Volunteer • Clean up your own mess • Be part of the solution • Give a compliment • Write a thank you note • Offer assistance • Hold the door open • Play by the rules • Put things back where they belong • Respect yourself and others • Lend a classmate a pencil

LOOKING FOR KINDNESS

(to the tune of "I've Been Working on the Railroad")

We've been looking for some kindness
all the live long day.
We've been looking for some kindness
just to make the world okay.
Kindness doesn't have to be hard
it's really easy to do.
Kindness once you get it started
Always comes back to you.

We've been looking for some kindness
All the live long day.
We've been looking for some kindness
just to make our school okay.
Kindness is as easy as sharing
no mean words from you.
Kindness once you get it started
always comes back to you.

KINDNESS MARCH

(rhythm of a military chant or jody)

I've got kindness every day
I've got kindness and that is okay.

I've got kindness in my heart
And I've got kindness and that makes me smart.

CHORUS
Kindness, 1,2
Kindness 3,4
Kindness 5,6,7,8
It's great!

I've got kindness in my class
I watch out for selfish acts.

I'm a kind person with my deeds
Now it's time for you to know,
kindness is the way to go!

REPEAT CHORUS

Kindness Pledge

Kindness matters!

I will be kind:

**in the words I speak,
in the way I treat people I know
and people I don't know.**

I will be kind to

**pets and other creatures in our world,
my family— brothers and sisters too.**

**I promise to show kindness
in big ways and small ways.
Because kindness matters;
it makes our world a better place.**

_____

The way I will start practicing kindness today

is_____.

Name:_____

Thumbs Up/Down for Kindness

INSTRUCTIONS:

Tell students they will be voting with their thumbs as to whether or not the situation you read shows kindness or not kindness.

Thumbs up—Kindness

Thumbs Down—Not kindness

Get your thumbs ready!

1. You noticed that someone in your class is always picked last for games. The next time it is your turn to pick, you pick them first.

2. The person next to you gets a bad grade on a spelling test and has to stay in at recess, and write his words. You make fun of him and call him "Stupid!"

3. Someone hurts your feelings at recess. When you come back in from recess you make a plan to get even and make her sorry she messed with you.

4. The new student in class doesn't know which table to sit at after he goes through the lunch line. You ask him to sit next to you.

5. You just got done painting the porch table for your mother. There is just a little paint left in the can. You realize it might make a mess in the garbage can if you put it in with paint in it. So you empty the little bit of paint that was left in the creek by your house.

6. You heard a person in your class has a pet that is sick and had to stay with the veterinarian. You notice this person walking all alone at recess and you invite him to play.

7. A person in your class makes a big mistake in gym and her team loses. You notice she look embarrassed and sad. You tell her not to worry about it; everyone messes up sometimes.

8. You are driving in the car with your family on vacation, everyone just finished with their lunch from the fast food restaurant. You volunteer to collect everyone's trash. Then you throw it out the window.

Reward them with Valentine's Day Applause for a job well done!

Activity Lesson: Kindness in Practice

MATERIALS NEEDED:

Heart cutouts, situations, glue, and a cute container from which to draw the situations.

INSTRUCTIONS:

1. Take the cutouts and glue the situations on them.

2. Laminate

SITUATIONS:

Someone is laughing at your friends because they answered a question wrong in class. Dad is fixing dinner for the family even though he doesn't feel well.

Your cat got into a fight with the neighbor's dog and has a deep cut.

Your little brother falls off his bike and skins his knee.

Your friend at school is sad because his dog ran away.

During gym the star basketball player who thinks he/she is "all that" misses the final point in the game, and your team loses.

Your sister feels bad because she didn't pass her test to get her driver's license.

At the end of the lesson have students come up, draw a situation and tell the class how they could practice kindness. Use Valentine's Day Applause to reward their participation.

Activity: How Can I Practice Kindness?

Use valentines to divide students into groups. Most boxes of valentines have 28-32 cards. Choose the name of the group from the verse on the front of the card. Example: You Can Count On Me, Valentine! Abbreviate this to the "You Can Count On Me Group." Have students answer the following questions;

How can I practice kindness in my classroom?

How can I practice kindness on the school bus?

How can I practice kindness at home?

How can I practice kindness to my pet?

How can I practice kindness in our community?

How can I practice kindness in our world?

How can I practice kindness to myself?

Students can then generate a list of ways to practice kindness. Have each group select a leader to report to the class. Let the group leader be the person with the longest little finger, smallest feet, longest finger nails, the tallest person in the group, etc. This is a way to allow someone to be selected as group leader randomly. Paper that the students record their responses on could be large paper hearts that you place on the board around the word kindness.

PROCESS THE ACTIVITY:

Ask the students what has to happen for any of these ideas to work. Respond that each of us has to do something to pass kindness along. "If it is to be, it is up to me!"

Bulletin Board Idea

VALENTINE'S DAY

MATERIALS NEEDED:
red fabric or red paper for background, newspaper, red construction paper, kindness suggestions printed

- ✿ Slogan for bulletin board: *Spread Kindness*

- ✿ Cover bulletin board in red fabric or red paper.

- ✿ For slogan use black letters, then cut out slightly larger letters of newspaper. Glue black letters on top of newspaper letters.

- ✿ Cut large hearts out of red construction paper and cut the same amount of larger hearts out of newspaper. Glue red hearts on top of newspaper hearts.

- ✿ By each heart have a suggestion for spreading kindness. Type these on your computer and back with newspaper in a slightly larger size rectangle.

SUGGESTIONS:

Do good

Use nice words

Be gentle

Smile at someone new

Share

Play fair

Think of others

Take turns

Help someone

VALENTINE ADVICE:
14 WAYS TO SHOW LOVE FOR YOUR CHILD
THIS VALENTINE'S DAY

- Use many positive words with your child.

- Respond promptly and lovingly to your child's physical and emotional needs and banish put-downs from your parent vocabulary.

- Make the effort to set a good example at home and in public. Use words like "I'm sorry," and "please."

- When your child is upset, argumentative or in a bad mood, give him a hug, cuddle, pat, secret sign or other affection he favors and talk with him about his feelings.

- Use non-violent forms of discipline. Parents should institute both rewards and restrictions many years before adolescence to help prevent trouble during the teenage years. Allowing children of any age to constantly break rules without being disciplined only encourages rule violations.

- Make plans to spend time alone with your young child or teen doing something she enjoys.

- Mark family game nights on your calendar so the entire family can be together. Put different family members under each date and have that person choose which game will be played that evening.

- Owning a pet can make children, especially those with chronic illness and disabilities, feel better by stimulating physical activity, enhancing over all attitude and offering constant companionship.

- One of the best ways to familiarize your child with good food choices is to encourage him to cook with you and to be involved in the entire process, from planning the menus to shopping for ingredients to the actual food preparation and serving.

- As your child grows up, she'll spend most of her time developing and refining a variety of skills and abilities. You should encourage her as much as possible.

- Your child's health depends significantly on the care and guidance you offer during his early years. By taking your child to the doctor regularly for consultations, keeping him safe from accidents, and providing a nutritious diet and opportunities for exercise throughout childhood, you protect and strengthen his body.

- Help your child develop positive relationships with friends, siblings and members of the community.

- One of your most important gifts as a parent is to help your child develop self-esteem. You child needs your support and encouragement to discover his strengths. He needs you to believe him as he learns to believe. Loving him, spending time with him, listening to him and praising his accomplishments are all part of this process.

- Don't forget to say, "I love you" to children of all ages!

Scrambled Words

KINDNESS

Name: _____ Class: _____ Date: _____

EACH SENTENCE HAS ONE WORD THAT IS SCRAMBLED. UNSCRAMBLE THAT WORD.

1. Being – – – – – – – – – – – for keeping
   your promises shows kindness.   oepirsslben

2. Being _ _ _ _ _ _ _ _ _ _ _ of others feelings
   shows kindness.   oisatncrdee

3. You show kindness when you are
   generous and _ _ _ _ _.   rhaes

4. Not making fun of another person who has
   made a mistake shows _ _ _ _ _ _ _ _ and kindness.   repetcs

5. Taking time to _ _ _ _ for your pet shows kindness.   reca

6. Kindness may be expressed by _ _ _ _ _ _ _
   as well as words.   iatscon

7. Kind people are _ _ _ _ _ _ people.   etilop

8. You show kindness when you
   are _ _ _ _ _ _ _ _ _ _ _ to others.   tmteycshipa

9. Treating others as you would like to
   be _ _ _ _ _ _ _ shows kindness.   tatdeer

10. Spreading _ _ _ _ _ _ _ _ makes you happy.   nisesndk

SELECT YOUR ANSWERS FROM THE FOLLOWING WORDS.
ANSWERS CAN BE FOUND ON PAGE 192.

sympathetic	responsible	share	considerate	polite
care	kindness	actions	treated	respect

Secret Code

KINDNESS

Name: _____ Class: _____ Date: _____

DECODE THE WORD IN EACH SENTENCE.

1. Kind people are _ _ _ _ _ _ people. — twghci

2. You show kindness when you are _ _ _ _ _ _ _ _ _ _ to others. — ezvtacsichb

3. Spreading _ _ _ _ _ _ _ _ makes you happy. — qhyryiee

4. Taking time to _ _ _ _ for your pet shows kindness. — bali

5. Being _ _ _ _ _ _ _ _ _ _ _ for keeping your promises shows kindness. — lietwyehjgi

6. Treating others as you would like to be _ _ _ _ _ _ _ shows kindness. — cliacir

7. You show kindness when you are generous and _ _ _ _ _. — esali

8. Not making fun of another person who has made a mistake shows _ _ _ _ _ _ _ and kindness. — lietibc

9. Kindness may be expressed by _ _ _ _ _ _ _ as well as words. — abchwye

10. Being _ _ _ _ _ _ _ _ _ _ _ of others feelings show kindness. — bwyehrilaci

SECRET CODE:

a	b	c	d	e	f	g	h	i	j	k	l	m	n	o	p	q	r	s	t	u	v	w	x	y	z
a	c	t	f	s	g	l	i	e	b	w	r	x	v	u	q	k	d	h	p	j	m	o	z	n	y

SELECT YOUR ANSWERS FROM THE FOLLOWING WORDS.
ANSWERS CAN BE FOUND ON PAGE 192.

actions	care	considerate	responsible	share
treated	sympathetic	kindness	respect	polite

Word Search

KINDNESS

Name: _____ Class: _____ Date: _____

TRY TO FIND THE HIDDEN WORDS.

```
U D K I N D Z V W P V V R H O C H R
Q W G S Y M P A T H E T I C J J C W
A C C O M M O D A T I N G C D V O L
J D S P L E A S A N T Y M U E C N M
T M H F G N Y I S P A B S K D R S P
H A A R N R X A O U O R H A I P I D
O N R I V B E K C K U L O Y C I D U
L N I E I W N G I M O T I V A T E D
I E N N G B S M A D S T U T T H R H
B R G D L E C P L R P F C H E U A J
D L E L Q N N A U N I Z S R D L T P
F Y J Y U E I E R W Y O Q J O G E W
E H Q Y I V K C R I D J U A M A V T
L A D R E O W Y E O N R S S M T X Y
U P Q K T L X B O V U G I W Q S P J
T P A G R E E A B L E S R E J I L G
B Y O B T N Y O I J P Z G Z Z P S O
Z Z W X O T R E S T R A B B T T S L
```

SELECT FROM THE FOLLOWING WORDS.
ANSWERS CAN BE FOUND ON PAGE 192.

nice	accommodating	caring	considerate
dedicated	gregarious	pleasant	sympathetic
polite	benevolent	agreeable	happy
kind	motivated	generous	friendly
social	mannerly	sharing	quiet

Answers

SCRAMBLED WORDS PAGE 189

1. responsible
2. considerate
3. share
4. respect
5. care
6. actions
7. polite
8. sympathetic
9. treated
10. kindness

SECRET CODE PAGE 190

1. polite
2. sympathetic
3. kindness
4. care
5. responsible
6. treated
7. share
8. respect
9. actions
10. considerate

WORD SEARCH PAGE 191

```
• • K I N D • • • • • • • • • • • •
• • • S Y M P A T H E T I C • • C •
A C C O M M O D A T I N G • D • O •
• • S P L E A S A N T • • • E • N •
• M H F G • • • S P • • • • D • S •
• A A R • R • • O • O • • • I • I •
• N R I • • E C • L • • • C • D •
• N I E • • • G I M O T I V A T E D
• E N N G B • • A • • • T • T • R •
• R G D • E C • L R • • • E • A •
• L • L Q N N A • • I • • • D • T •
• Y • Y U E I E R • • O • • • • E •
• H • • I V • C R I • • U • • • • •
• A • • E O • • E O N • • S • • • •
• P • • T L • • • U G • • • • • • •
• P A G R E E A B L E S • • • • • •
• Y • • • N • • • • • • • • • • • •
• • • • • T • • • • • • • • • • • •
```

April Fool's Day
A SENSE OF HUMOR

Introduction

APRIL FOOL'S DAY
A SENSE OF HUMOR

In most countries around the world April 1st is called All Fools' Day. It received its name from the custom of playing practical jokes. This day has been observed for many centuries, but there are different explanations for the celebration. The customs surrounding the celebration resemble the holiday or festival of Hilaria of ancient Rome, held on March 25th, and the Holi celebration in India which ends on March 31st. Our modern April Fool's Day may have started in France, in 1582, with the Gregorian calendar moving New Year's Day from March 25th to January 1st. It is thought that some continued to celebrate the end of the year on April 1st, and these people who continued this tradition were called fools. The tradition may also be related to the vernal equinox, March 21, when people are said to be fooled by the sudden changes in the weather.

There are differences how the various countries celebrate April Fool's Day but all have the common theme of making a person play the fool. In France the person being fooled is called poisson d'avril ("April fish"). It is felt the French are referring to a young fish that is easily caught. In France school children pin a paper fish to the backs of other unsuspecting students. In Scotland the day is called Gowkie Day for the gowk or cuckoo. In some countries newspapers have been known to join in by printing false headlines or news stories.

Playing pranks and practical jokes on people are the tradition of April Fool's Day. It takes a good sense of humor to be the recipient of a practical joke. A sense of humor is what makes life fun, and there are few pleasures that rival sharing a good laugh with a child. A sense of humor can brighten your day, help you handle a difficult situation and not let you take yourself too seriously. Our life lesson for this holiday is the importance of having a sense of humor.

Ways To Use Humor In The Classroom

Lighthearted humor can bring twinkles to the eyes, groans and chuckles from your students. Here are some ideas to consider:

- Tell a joke to your class. If it bombs, don't worry or get embarrassed. Don't try to explain the joke; just tell them "That is why I keep my day job!" The students will love the fact that you tried. And telling jokes will get easier.

- Convey your sense of humor through the clothes and accessories you use. Accessorize your lesson themes with amusing hats, funny ties, watches, scarves or sweaters.

- As easy source of humor to share is the comic section of the newspaper. Read it with a keen eye attuned to the areas where you may work it into your curriculum.

- Use bells, whistles or funny noisemakers as a signal to get your students' attention.

- Most classes have at least one student who is witty and spur of the moment.

Play a straight man to his or her comic routine, without letting it become disruptive or out of control.

- When a lesson isn't going well, pick up an object in your classroom and start softly talking or whispering to it to get the students' attention. Or to introduce a lesson, pull out a picture of the famous person related to the lesson and start having a conversation with him or her.

- Share humorous books, poems, quotations and jokes with your class. Set aside a special time of the day to do this.

- Plan humorous bulletin boards and learning centers and select humorous posters for your room.

Suggested book to read to learn more ways of infusing humor in the classroom—*Comedy Real Life: A Guide to Helping Kids Survive in an Imperfect World* by Emily Oldak

April Fool's Day

LESSON—A SENSE OF HUMOR

OBJECTIVES:

At the end of the lesson the students will be able to explain a custom of April Fool's Day.

At the end of the lesson the students will be able to explain why having a good sense of humor is important.

At the end of the lesson the students will be able to explain how to develop a sense of humor.

MATERIALS NEEDED:

Overhead projector, overheads, activity materials, song lyrics, follow up activity and story.

"CHUCKLES" APPLAUSE:

Clap hands once in front of you. Then hold stomach and laugh three times. Why "Chuckles Applause?" Because having a sense of humor is important.

OPTIONAL MATERIALS:

Open the lesson with the Cole Porter song, Be A Clown, this song is on the soundtrack from the movie, De-Lovely, about Porter's life.

1. Open the lesson with the background about April Fools' Day. Adjust the material you are sharing to the age of the students to whom you are presenting.

   ### OPTIONAL OPENING

   play the song for the class and ask what the song describes that the world loves and why. Use "Chuckles" Applause to reward the students.

2. Share with the students that it is important to have a sense of humor when people tease you, try to bully you or play practical jokes on you.

3. Use the overheads in the following order:

   🌴 A Sense of Humor

   🌴 More Reasons... *Use the Group Activity at this point of the lesson. Use "Chuckles" Applause to reward the students.*

   🌴 How would you?

   🌴 How do you develop a sense of humor? *After this read the story that you have selected. Discuss how humor is related or how it would have helped the situation based on the story you selected.*

   🌴 Quotes about humor

   🌴 Top Ten Reasons to Have a Sense of Humor

4. End the lesson by reminding the students how important it is to have a sense of humor. Leave a follow up activity with the teacher.

APRIL FOOL'S DAY

It's April Fools' Day—Steven Kroll

April Fools' Day—Melissa Schiller

Arthur's April Fool—Mark Brown

Mud Flat April Fool—James Stevenson.

TEASING

Simon's Hook—Karen Gedig Burnett

The Berenstain Bears and Too Much Teasing—Stan and Jan Berenstain

Yanni Rubbish—Shulamith Levey

Gakky Two-Feet—Micky Dolenz

If the Shoe Fits—Gary Soto

Just Kidding—Trudy Ludwig

TEASING (VIDEOS & DVD'S)

Buddy Learns About Teasing—Boulden Publishing

Sticks and Stones—Boulden Publishing

LESSONS WITH HUMOR

Gerald McBoing Boing—Dr. Seuss

Green Eggs and Ham—Dr. Seuss

The Lorax—Dr. Seuss

Fox in Socks—Dr. Seuss

The Sneetches—Dr. Seuss

HUMOROUS STORIES

Silly Sally—Audrey Wood

How Are You Peeling?—Joost Elffers

Imogene's Antlers—David Small

Please Bury Me In the Library—J. Patrick Lewis

The Mysterious Tadpole—Steven Kellogg

A Sense of Humor...

IS VERY IMPORTANT BECAUSE...

Being able to laugh at yourself when you make a mistake (we all make mistakes) helps you not to take yourself so seriously and lowers your stress!

Being able to make a joke of another student's teasing helps the teasing to stop because it is not any fun to tease someone who doesn't get mad, red in the face or look like they are going to cry.

Being able to make a joke or laugh off a situation with a bully can help make the bully lose interest in you. It is not any fun to bully someone who doesn't act mad, get red in the face or act like they are going to cry.

More Reasons...

A SENSE OF HUMOR IS VERY IMPORTANT!

Being able to laugh with people, friends and family in your life and not at people, friends and family helps you connect with them and have a better relationship. Sharing funny and amusing moments in life connects people.

Having a sense of humor with yourself, friends and family will make you a pleasant person to be around and spend time with.

Being able to laugh about life and situations you find yourself in helps you adapt and adjust to all sorts of life experiences.

How would you use humor if...?

Someone called you "four eyes"
because you wear glasses.

You have a birthmark on your leg and
kids tease you that you got a tattoo.

Someone called you a big fat pig.

Someone called you a "retard" because
you go to the multi-handicapped unit
in your school and read to the students.

Someone made fun of your parent's job
because you don   t have a really large house
and new clothes like the other students.

Someone made fun of your science
report about frogs; they said you
look like your science report!

How do you develop a sense of humor?

🌵 *Learn to laugh at yourself when you do something silly.*

🌵 **Laugh with important people in your life when they gently tease you and mean you no harm.**

🌵 *Read jokes and humorous stories and poems.*

🌵 **Practice changing teasing and bullying situations by using humor.**

🌵 *NEVER, NEVER, NEVER use humor in a mean-spirited way, with off-color jokes or racial slurs.*

Quotes About Humor

QUOTES ABOUT HUMOR FROM SOME OF OUR FAVORITE PEOPLE:

"From there to here, from here to there, funny things are everywhere."

Dr. Seuss

"Laugh and the world laughs with you. Cry and you simply get wet."

Cliff Thomas

"If it were not for my little jokes, I could not bear the burdens of this office."

Abraham Lincoln

"You grow up the day you have your first really good laugh at yourself."

Ethel Barrymore

Top Ten Reasons to Have a Sense of Humor

1. It helps you not to take yourself too seriously.

2. You don't get sick as often.

3. You have less stress.

4. You are less likely to be depressed and sad.

5. It helps you see another point of view.

6. It makes you more spontaneous and that makes you more interesting.

7. It helps you think in creative ways, adults call it "thinking outside the box!"

8. It helps you put life into perspective and to see beyond what is happening right now.

9. It helps you have high self-esteem.

10. It helps you handle teasing, bullies and other mean people.

Song

I'VE BEEN WORKING ON MY SENSE OF HUMOR
Sung to the Tune of I've Been Working On the Railroad

I've been working on my sense of humor
All the live long day.
I've been working on my sense of humor
Just to make my day okay.
A sense of humor is important it helps in everything you do.
Laughing will help you feel better
It helps get you through.

I've been working on my sense of humor
All the live long day.
I've been working on my sense of humor
Just to make the teasing go away.
A sense of humor is important it helps in everything you do.
Chuckling will help you feel better
It helps get you through.

I've been working on my sense of humor
All the live long day.
I've been working on my sense of humor
Just to make the bullies go away.
A sense of humor is important it helps in everything you do
Giggling will help you feel better
It helps get you through.

Group Lesson: Comic Strips and Cartoons

Use comics and cartoons from the daily paper to teach critical thinking skills. Starting several weeks in advance read the daily comic strips and political cartoons and select those cartoons which teach about handling a life situation with humor. Remember political cartoons are not always about politics. Cut them out and start making a file. This activity will be having the students analyze and discuss and giving them ideas for their own creation of a cartoon or comic strip. Or if you want to purchase a book of cartoons consider *School Cartoon Series* compiled by Dave Craig, Paperbacks for Educators. Also check the internet for cartoon websites.

MATERIALS NEEDED:

cartoons for each group to analyze.

INSTRUCTIONS:

- Divide students into the following group names: Funny Bones, Laughing All the Way, Snicker Here and Snicker There, Giggle Buddies, Chuckle Luckles. The group leader will be the student with the smallest pinky finger.

- Distribute the cartoons or comics. Ask the students to read the comic strip or cartoon and analyze what is being said and if it is using humor to get a point across. Group leader will report back to class.

- Group leader reports back to class about the group's cartoon or comic strip. Have the whole group pop up and reward them with "Chuckles Applause" as described in the lesson.

Craft: Comic Strip

HOW TO HANDLE TEASING, LIFE AND BULLIES

Students will be creating their own cartoon strips on how to handle teasing, life and bullies with a sense of humor. The students may choose their own situations, but the cartoon must show humor in handling the situation.

MATERIALS NEEDED:

large sheets of white paper that you have cut lengthwise into two long strips and colored pencils markers or crayons.

INSTRUCTIONS:

- Explain to the students that they will be creating their own comic strip to show how to handle a teasing, life or bully situation using a sense of humor. They may create their own name for the comic strip.

- Distribute a long strip of white paper to each child. Explain to the students that they may divide the paper into different frames to depict different scenes in their comic strip. They may use colored pencils, markers or crayons.

- Display the comic strips in the hallway or on a bulletin board.

A SENSE OF HUMOR

A sense of humor can brighten any family's life. When you laugh with someone it is a way of connecting with that person. A good sense of humor can also make your children smarter, healthier and better able to cope with challenges like teasing and bullying. You can help your child learn a sense of humor. A sense of humor can assist your child in these ways:

- See situations from another perspective.

- Be spontaneous.

- Understand creative ideas and out of the box ways of thinking.

- Be able to see beyond the surface of a situation.

- Enjoy and participate in the humorous aspects of life.

- Not take himself or herself too seriously.

There are ways to help develop your child's sense of humor. Here are some suggestions:

- Be a good role model- Use your own sense of humor. Make jokes, tell funny stories, laugh out loud and don't take yourself too seriously.

- Encourage your own child's sense of humor.

- Make humor a part of your everyday life. You share your own funny observations or reactions to life situations.

- Draw the line on inappropriate or mean spirited or off color jokes.

- Encourage the whole family to laugh together. Humor is social and that is why you probably laugh louder and harder at a humorous situation in a movie because people surround you.

A sense of humor is what makes life fun. There are few pleasures that rival sharing a good laugh with your child.

"Laughter is internal jogging."

William Fry

Crossword Puzzle

A SENSE OF HUMOR

Name: _____ Class: _____ Date: _____

FILL IN THE CROSSWORD PUZZLE BY USING THE CLUES.

ACROSS:

1. Having a good sense of humor helps you have high _ _ _ _ _ _ _ _ _ _.
2. People with a sense of humor are _ _ _ _ _ _ _ _ to be around.
3. A sense of humor helps you see _ _ _ _ _ _ _ point of view.
4. A sense of humor imporves your _ _ _ _ _ _ _ _ _ _ _ _ with people.
5. You are less likely to be sad and depressed if you have a _ _ _ _ sense of humor.

DOWN:

1. A sense of humor helps you handle _ _ _ _ _ _ _.
2. Always laught with _ _ _ _ _ _ not at them.
3. You have less _ _ _ _ _ _ when you have a sense of humor.
4. Having a snese of humor helps you not take _ _ _ _ _ _ _ _ so seriously.
5. It is important to be able to _ _ _ _ _ at yourself.

SELECT YOUR ANSWERS FROM THE FOLLOWING WORDS.
ANSWERS CAN BE FOUND ON PAGE 211.

stress	self-esteem	good	people	laugh
teasing	another	relationship	pleasant	yourself

Secret Code

A SENSE OF HUMOR

Name: _____ Class: _____ Date: _____

DECODE THE WORD IN EACH SENTENCE.

1. It is important to be able to _ _ _ _ _ at yourself. svwki

2. People with a sense of humor are
   _ _ _ _ _ _ _ _ to be around. qsyvzvmn

3. Always laught with _ _ _ _ _ _ not at them. qyoqsy

4. Having a good sense of humor helps
   you have high _ _ _ _ _ _ _ _ _ _ _. zysayznyyr

5. A sense of humor improves your
   _ _ _ _ _ _ _ _ _ _ _ _ _ with people. dysvnfomzifqz

6. A sense of humor helps you
   handle _ _ _ _ _ _ _. nyvzfmk

7. You have less _ _ _ _ _ _ when
   you have a sense of humor. zndyzz

8. You are less likely to be sad and depressed
   if you have a _ _ _ _ sense of humor. kooh

9. A sense of humor helps you see
   _ _ _ _ _ _ _ point of view. vmoniyd

10. Having a snese of humor helps you
    not take _ _ _ _ _ _ _ _ so seriously. bowdzysa

SECRET CODE:

a b c d e f g h i j k l m n o p q r s t u v w x y z
f y b r w i z d h k g c n t o x p m l j q a u v e s

SELECT YOUR ANSWERS FROM THE FOLLOWING WORDS.
ANSWERS CAN BE FOUND ON PAGE 211.

yourself	relationships	teasing	laugh	pleasant
self-esteem	people	another	good	stress

Word Search

Name: _____ Class: _____ Date: _____

TRY TO FIND THE HIDDEN WORDS.

```
Q E U Y X D A J W A P N K D C R N Q
G Y S S B U N J Q A D U Y N T H B N
Y G E E E O C Y D Z N G L P R R R
N O R W L L T B G R I Y U J B J N G
Q O Q Z V F H G B E Y T U M K J Q T
R D Y S T R E S S D P O S S K P K H
E M T O E I R S L G Q S G G N B I B
L N E U U P M O T M P O Y N N H P W
A M A M N R S X X E L Y S V N U P B
T O S I W E S Z T X E V Q R J V O D
I Y I X E F G E B F A M E M T D F S
O U N Z P E O P L E S D H W H I F I
N R G F V E U D A F A B F V E I R U
S T F F C X C V U X N U I W U K B B
H R B C G L M I G Y T Q Y I P E J I
I F H T S D M J H R D G Y M C J D M
P E Y A I X C M A A U L G N K C L Z
S C E P F O W Q V A P Y S T A S I T
```

SELECT FROM THE FOLLOWING WORDS.
ANSWERS CAN BY FOUND ON PAGE 211.

| pleasant | teasing | another | stress | people |
| relationships | self-esteem | yourself | good | laugh |

Answers

Secret Code page 209

1. laugh
2. pleasant
3. people
4. self-esteem
5. relationships
6. teasing
7. stress
8. good
9. another
10. yourself

Crossword Puzzle page 208

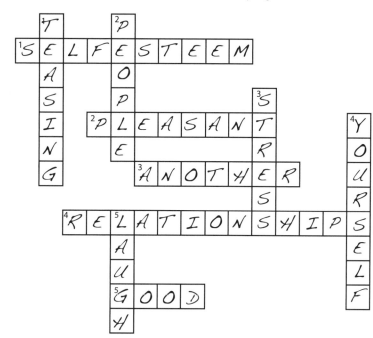

Word Search page 210

```
· · · · · · A · · · · · · · · ·
· · S · · · N · · · · · · · · · ·
· G · E · · O · · · · · · · · · ·
· O · · L · T · · · · · · · · · ·
· O · · · F H · · · · · · · · · ·
R D Y S T R E S S · · · · · · · ·
E · T O · · R S · · · · · · · · ·
L · E · U · · · T · P · · · · · ·
A · A · · R · · · E L · · · · · ·
T · S · · · S · · · E · · · · · ·
I · I · · · · E · · A M · · · · ·
O · N · P E O P L E S · · · · · ·
N · G · · · · A F A · · · · · · ·
S · · · · · · U · N · · · · · · ·
H · · · · · · G · T · · · · · · ·
I · · · · · · H · · · · · · · · ·
P · · · · · · · · · · · · · · · ·
S · · · · · · · · · · · · · · · ·
```

Chapter Twelve

Mother's Day
&
Father's Day
GRATITUDE

Mother's Day & Father's Day

GRATITUDE

Who started the traditional celebrations of Mother's and Father's Day?

Both of these started with a very special mother and father.

MOTHER'S DAY

In the United States Mother's Day is celebrated on the second Sunday in May. Many other countries in the world also celebrate the holiday on this date, while some countries celebrate the holiday at different times in the calendar year. In the Middle Ages the custom developed of allowing those who had moved away from their home parishes to visit on the fourth Sunday of Lent. This became Mothering Sunday in Britain. This tradition continued into modern times but has largely been replaced by Mother's Day. In ancient times festivals honoring mothers and mother goddesses were held. Some countries have continued to observe these ancient festivals. In India the festival of Durgapuja honoring the goddess Durga remains an important festival.

Anna Jarvis grew up in the state of West Virginia shortly after the Civil War ended in 1865. During this period of history, there was a lot of disagreement between members of some families because soldiers from the same family might have been on different sides of the Civil War. Anna's mother wished there were a holiday called Mother's Day. Her mother believed that brothers would make peace with each other on their mother's special day. Anna's mother, Mrs. Anna Jarvis, organized women's groups to promote friendship and health. When Anna became older, she carried out her mother's wishes. She held a Memorial Service in her late mother's church in Grafton, West Virginia, on May 12, 1907, which became the first Mother's Day. Anna spread the idea of Mother's Day, and it became popular. She wrote to world leaders asking them to make Mother's Day an official holiday. In 1914, President Woodrow Wilson made it a national holiday. Jarvis promoted the idea of wearing a white carnation to give tribute to one's mother. Over time the tradition of giving gratitude and thanks to mothers expanded to include grandmothers, aunts and others who played mothering roles in young lives.

FATHER'S DAY

In the United States, Father's Day is celebrated on the third Sunday in June. Some Roman Catholics have continued to observe the feast day of Saint Joseph on March 19 as a tribute to fathers. The originator of Father's Day was a woman named Sonora Smart Dodd. She was inspired by Mother's Day and wanted to have a holiday to honor fathers. It is said that she was inspired to start the holiday by listening to a Mother's Day sermon in 1909. Dodd's father was a Civil War veteran who raised her and five siblings after their mother died in childbirth. When she proposed the idea local religious leaders supported it and the first Father's Day was celebrated on June 19, 1910. This was the month of Dodd's father's birthday. President Calvin Coolidge gave his support to the holiday in 1924, and in 1966 President Lyndon B. Johnson officially proclaimed it a national holiday. The observance was decreed by law in 1972. Some people observe the holiday by wearing a red rose to signify that one's father is living or a white rose to indicate that he is deceased.

MOTHER'S DAY AND FATHER'S DAY

LESSON—GRATITUDE

OBJECTIVES:

⚜ At the end of the lesson the students will be able to explain why Mother's Day and Father's Day originated.

⚜ At the end of the lesson the students will be able to explain what gratitude is.

⚜ At the end of the lesson the students will be able to list ways to express gratitude.

MATERIALS NEEDED:

Overhead projector, overheads, story or skit, worksheet one for each student and follow up activity for the teacher.

"SHINE YOUR HALO APPLAUSE"

Clap once in front of you then take your right hand and circle above like you are shining your halo. Why "Shine Your Halo Applause?" Because that what gets shined when you express gratitude for the people, things, pets and events in your life.

1. Open the lesson with background information about the holiday you are teaching. Be sensitive to and point out to the student's that the role of mother and father can be filled by many significant adults in their lives; many students are parented by aunts, uncles, grandparents etc. Adjust the information to the grade level of your students.

2. Tell them on this holiday it is important to express gratitude to those important people in their lives.

3. Use the overheads to present the lesson on gratitude in this order:

⚜ Gratitude is… If you are using the worksheet, do that activity now.

⚜ What are some things we are grateful for? If you are using a story or the skit, do that activity now. Be sure to use "Shine Your Halo Applause" to praise students for their responses. Discuss with students how gratitude was shown in the story or skit.

⚜ How would you express gratitude if?

⚜ Gratitude Pledge

4. End lesson by reminding the students how important it is to express gratitude in their lives.

Books

GRATITUDE

The Secret of Saying Thanks—Douglas Wood

The Most Thankful Thing—Lisa Mccourt

Thanks & Giving: All Year Long—Marlo Thomas

I Never Say I'm Thankful, But I Am—Jane Belk Moncure

I Got a Family—Melrose Cooper

Jafta's Mother—Hugh Lewin

Jafata's Father—Hugh Lewin

Grandpa, Me and Our House in the Tree—Barbara Kirk

Giving Thanks: A Native American Good Morning Message—
   Chief Jake Swamp

Twenty and Ten—Claire H. Bishop

MOTHER'S DAY

The Mother's Day Mice—Eve Bunting

Henry Mudge and the Funny Lunch—
   Cynthia Rylant

*The Berenstain Bears and the Mama's Day
   Surprise*—Stan and Jan Berenstain

Mother's Mother's Day—Lorna Balian

A Chair for My Mother—Verna b. Williams

Happy Mother's Day, Mami!—Leslie Valdes

My Mother's Voice—Joanne Ryder

FATHER'S DAY

My Father's Hands—Joanne Ryder

A Perfect Father's Day—Eve Bunting

The Secret Father's Day Present—
   Andrew Clements

It's Father's Day Charlie Brown!—
   Judy Katschke (adapter)

I Love My Daddy—Sebastien Braun

What is Father's Day?—Harriet Ziefert

Happy Father's Day—Steve Kroll

Gratitude is...

Gratitude is appreciating what you have.

There are many words that describe gratitude:

Appreciation ...."Thank you so much!"

Thankful ...."I am so grateful for what you did!"

Indebted ...."I owe you one!"

Obliged ...."If you ever need anything, just call on me!"

But gratitude is...

When you are thankful for the people in
your life, the events that happen to you and
those small and big things that happen everyday.

Gratitude is...

When you don't take people, events
and things in your life for granted.

There are many ways to express gratitude, you express gratitude when you:

Say thank you!

When you take care of our world.

When you appreciate people in your life and let them know.

When you appreciate yourself for your uniqueness and individual talents and don't compare yourself with others.

When you spend time with special people, things and pets in your life.

When you really listen to people when they share stories and important life events.

How would you express gratitude if:

1. Someone complimented you on good teamwork in your last game?

2. A classmate expressed that they wished they were as talented as you?

3. Your friend stopped by to see why you missed school.

4. Your mother got the grass stain out of your new soccer uniform just in time for team pictures.

5. Your grandfather asked you to come over on Saturday and spend time with him.

6. Your dad told you he was proud you were his child.

7. You were asked to participate in a neighborhood clean up day.

8. You had the choice of helping clean out the garage with mom or not helping.

My Gratitude Pledge

I
promise
upon my honor,
to always be grateful
for
the people, pets, things and events
in my life.
I will always express
my thankfulness
to those
I
treasure
so
they will know
how much
they mean to me.

Craft: Gratitude Coupon Book

Using the template below have your students make a coupon booklet for the important people in their lives to whom they wish to show appreciation. On the board write or make an overhead of this page to give suggestions as to what your students might be willing to do to show appreciation and gratitude to those important people in their lives. Make duplicate copies of the template to generate multiple copies of the "gratitude coupon" for your students.

WAYS TO SHOW APPRECIATION:

Clean my room without being asked.

Not bug you when you are tired.

Do my homework without being asked.

Spend time with you.

Not be in a bad mood for 3 days.

5 free hugs whenever needed.

Read a story to my brothers and sisters.

Give the dog a bath.

Listen to your advice when you talk to me.

Take out the trash.

Say Thank-you!

Set the table.

Pay attention to you.

Wash the dishes.

Help you work!

Help clean out the garage

Give 5 compliments whenever you need them.

Entertain my younger brothers and sisters when you are tired.

Pick up my toys without being asked.

Gratitude Coupon

May be redeemed at any time. ~ No expiration date.

To: _____ ~ For: _____

You are special and I appreciate you!

_____   _____
Signature   Date

TOPIC:

Showing gratitude to people in your life

Sometimes we take those who mean the most to us for granted. In this skit, students will reflect on those special people in their lives and all that they do for them. The character Alana finds her aunt suddenly sick and in the hospital and realizes by her absence how much her aunt does for her and the family. The skit will also promote discussion of how we can show the special people in our lives how much we appreciate them.

CHARACTERS:

Alana, Gurpreet, and Ben

SETTING:

Walking Home From School

Alana, Gurpreet and Ben are walking home from school. Alana looks a little sad and depressed, so her friends try to cheer her up.

ALANA: I wish I could go swimming. My uncle said I have to go straight home after school. Mrs. Valdez is babysitting us, and my uncle doesn't want me to leave while she is there.

GURPREET: My step-dad would be happy to give you a ride if that is the problem. We drive right by your house.

ALANA: I wish that was the only problem that would be easy to solve. But it doesn't have anything to do with needing a ride. My uncle said that since he needs to go to the hospital to visit my aunt, when I am at home he doesn't have to worry about where I am.

BEN: He probably doesn't want to worry about anything happening to you. One family member in the hospital at a time is enough.

ALANA: I suppose you are right, but I never realized how much my aunt did for me until she got sick. Last night we ate chili for the third night in a row. Tonight my uncle promised he would make something different. I am hoping for spaghetti.

GURPREET: Is Mrs. Valdez nice?

ALANA: I think she tries to be nice but she doesn't let me watch half the TV shows my aunt does; and she is always checking what I am doing on the computer. Then when I get a phone call, she doesn't let me stay on the phone very long. I miss my aunt!

GURPREET: Why don't you ask your uncle to talk to her?

ALANA: I tried that already. He said just to put up with it a little longer. Getting a sitter is hard, and he doesn't want to "rock the boat."

BEN: Hey, maybe tomorrow you could come to my house. My little sister would love to see you. That would give you a vacation from Mrs. Valdez.

ALANA: I appreciate the invitation, but I might get to go to the hospital tomorrow to visit my aunt. I will ask my uncle about it for the next day though if the invitation still stands.

BEN: Great, I'll ask my mom to fix chocolate cake tomorrow. That is your favorite, right?

ALANA: Would you? That would be great!

GURPREET: And I will ask if you can come to my house the next night.

ALANA: This is terrific! If I can hang out at your houses until my aunt is out of the hospital, maybe it won't be so bad.

GURPREET: Tomorrow is spirit day at school. We are all supposed to wear our school shirts. Don't forget to do that.

ALANA: Uhh… I don't think so. Mine is still dirty from last Friday when I slide into home in gym class and got mud all over it. We haven't done the laundry since my aunt went to the hospital; my uncle hasn't had time. I never realized how much I took for granted what my aunt did.

GURPREET: Why don't Ben and I come over and help you do the laundry? It is not that hard. Both of us know how to do laundry.

ALANA: But I don't know how to sort clothes or run the washing machine!

BEN: I know how, plus all you have to do is read the instructions and know the difference between dark and white clothes. And don't ever put red clothes in either one of those loads. Wash red clothes by themselves! Besides if I don't know what to do, I can call my mother.

GURPREET: Or I'm sure Mrs. Valdez will help us!

ALANA: Okay, I never realized how much stuff my aunt takes care of at our house. I even miss her bugging me to finish my homework and clean my room. I guess some good can come out of a bad situation. Thanks a lot guys.

BEN: Anytime!

GURPREET: If you can't count on your family and good friends, who can you count on?

Gratitude Profile

INSTRUCTIONS:

Each character statement below is based on the theme of being grateful.
Rank each character statement as you feel it appears in your life.

CHARACTER STATEMENT	NEVER									ALWAYS
1. I appreciate the things of nature	1 2 3 4 5 6 7 8 9 10									
2. My friends know I appreciate them	1 2 3 4 5 6 7 8 9 10									
3. I spent time with my family and loved ones.	1 2 3 4 5 6 7 8 9 10									
4. I always wish I had what other people have.	1 2 3 4 5 6 7 8 9 10									
5. I always tell my people thank you when they help me, do something nice for me or spend time with me.	1 2 3 4 5 6 7 8 9 10									
6. I am envious of people who have more talent than me.	1 2 3 4 5 6 7 8 9 10									
7. I take time to think about what is good in my life.	1 2 3 4 5 6 7 8 9 10									
8. I make choices to take care of myself and my body.	1 2 3 4 5 6 7 8 9 10									
9. I seldom take time to listen to my grandparents' stories.	1 2 3 4 5 6 7 8 9 10									
10. I participate in community and school projects to help people who are in need.	1 2 3 4 5 6 7 8 9 10									

REVIEW YOUR ANSWERS. IF YOU HAVE QUESTIONS THAT YOU HAVE RATED 1-5,
WORK ON IMPROVING THESE AREAS IN YOUR LIFE.

GRATITUDE

Sung to the tune of This Old Man

Gratitude is important,
It is very, very important,
Because it shows the people that you care,
And you appreciate what they do!

Thankfulness is like gratitude,
It is when you show appreciation
For the people, events and things
that are in your life.
It shows that you care about these, too.

Gratitude is important,
It is very, very important,
Because it shows the people that you care,
And you appreciate what they do!

Thumbs Up/Down for Gratitude

INSTRUCTIONS:

Tell students they will be voting with their thumbs as to whether or not the situation you read shows kindness or no kindness.

THUMBS UP—BEING GRATEFUL!

THUMBS DOWN—NOT BEING GRATEFUL!

Get your thumbs ready!

1. Your Dad tells you how proud he is of you when you finish your soccer game. You don't say anything because you are too mad about missing the goal.

2. You hear at school that a classmate's mother was injured in a serious accident at the place she worked. You start to think about how lucky you are to have a wonderful stepmom and when you get home from school you tell her how much you appreciate what she does for you.

3. Your mom's boyfriend has volunteered to fill in for your baseball coach while she is recovering from surgery. You tell him thanks because this means your team can continue with the season's games.

4. Your aunt is always winning awards and traveling to foreign countries. You are envious of her success and talent.

5. You win first place in the school district's science fair. You say to yourself, "that was so easy I will win next year's competition too."

6. Every day when you get up, your stepdad has breakfast made and your lunch packed for school. He also takes time to chaperon your class's overnight trip to Camp Kern. You think, "No big deal; I'm sure everyone's step-dad does the same."

7. You broke your arm in gym class. That evening your friend stops by to check on you. You say, "Thanks for caring about me."

8. Your mentor takes time off from work to see you perform in your class play. You tell them how much you appreciate the fact that he came and that he took time to be interested in what you do.

Game: Pass the Gratitude!

In this game no one wants to hold "the gratitude—the game's only prop. To begin you select a student to be "it." That person holds the gratitude. The game caller you or the classroom teacher, says to the person holding the object, "Name five ways to say thank you. Pass the gratitude!" The students quickly pass the object to the right. Students quickly pass the object around the circle. If it returns to the original holder before they can name all five ways to say thank you, the holder is still "it." Otherwise the person holding the object when the situations are named is it.

MATERIALS:

an object such as a Frisbee, ball or hat. You could also use a bean bag. Game statements.

STATEMENTS:

1. Name five ways to say thank you.
2. Name five ways to praise someone.
3. Name five ways to appreciate your friends.
4. Name five ways to appreciate yourself.
5. Name five people for whom to be grateful.
6. Name five people in your family or school for whom to be grateful.
7. Name five people in the community for whom to be grateful.
8. Name five things in your world for whom to be grateful.
9. Name five ways to appreciate your pet.
10. Name five ways to show your teacher you are grateful for him/her.
11. Name five ways to show appreciation on the school bus.
12. Name five ways to spend positive time with your family.
13. Name five people who do jobs in our community for whom you are grateful.
14. Name five ways to show your pet you are grateful for him/her.
15. Name five ways to show our world you are grateful for it.
16. Name five people who help you stay healthy for whom you are grateful.
17. Name five positive things at school or in your life for which you are grateful.
18. Name five experiences, people or things for which you are grateful in gym class.
19. Name five things for which you are grateful that the principal does for our school.
20. Name five things for which you are grateful that our school custodians do.
21. Name five things for which you are grateful that our cafeteria workers do.
22. Name five things for which you are grateful in music class.
23. Name five things for which you are grateful in art class.
24. Name five things for which you are grateful that our student council does.
23. Name five things for which you are grateful that the President of the United States does.

Bulletin Board Idea

"Gratitude is giving thanks for special people and things in your life."

MATERIALS NEEDED:

flower cut-outs, or you may make your own from construction paper, blue fabric or paper to cover the board, complementary border that accents your flowers, words printed in large font on your computer to place in the center of the flowers and black letters to spell out the above heading for the bulletin board.

INSTRUCTIONS:

- Cover the bulletin board with blue paper or fabric, attach border and gratitude quote in black letters.

- Attach flowers varying the height of the stems.

- Attach ways to praise words to the center of the flowers.

WAYS TO PRAISE:

Thank you!

I appreciate you!

You're the best!

Helping!

Spending time together!

MOTHER'S AND FATHER'S DAY

Who started the traditional celebrations of Mother's and Father's Day?

Both of these started with a very special mother and father.

Anna Jarvis grew up in the state of West Virginia shortly after the Civil War ended in 1865. During this period of history there was a lot of disagreement between members of some families because soldiers from the same family might have been on different sides of the Civil War. Anna's mother wished there were a holiday called Mother's Day. Her mother believed that brothers would make peace with each other on their mother's special day. Anna's mother, Mrs. Anna Jarvis, organized women's groups to promote friendship and health. When Anna became older, she carried out her mother's wishes. She held a Memorial Service in her late mother's church in Grafton, West Virginia, on May 12, 1907, which became the first Mother's Day. Anna spread the idea of Mother's Day, and it became popular. She wrote to world leaders asking them to make Mother's Day an official holiday. In 1914, President Woodrow Wilson made it a national holiday. Jarvis promoted the idea of wearing a white carnation to give tribute to one's mother. Over time the tradition of giving gratitude and thanks to mothers has expanded to include grandmothers, aunts and others who have played mothering roles in young lives.

The originator of Father's Day was a woman named Sonora Smart Dodd. She was inspired by Mother's Day, and wanted to have a holiday to honor fathers. It is said that she was inspired to start the holiday by listening to a Mother's Day sermon in 1909. Dodd's father was a Civil War veteran who raised her and five siblings after their mother died in childbirth. When she proposed the idea, local religious leaders supported it and the first Father's Day was celebrated on June 19, 1910. This was the month of Dodd's father's birthday. President Calvin Coolidge gave his support to the holiday in 1924, and in 1966 President Lyndon B. Johnson officially proclaimed it a national holiday. The observance was decreed by law in 1972. Some people observe the holiday by wearing a red rose to signify that one's father is living or a white rose to indicate that he is deceased.

Crossword Puzzle

GRATITUDE

Name: _____ Class: _____ Date: _____

FILL IN THE CROSSWORD PUZZLE BY USING THE CLUES.

ACROSS:

1. It is _ _ _ _ _ _ _ _ _ not to take people for granted.

2. Gratitude is being _ _ _ _ _ _ _ _ for things others do for you.

3. You should be _ _ _ _ _ _ _ _ for people who take care of you.

4. Parents, food, clothes, toys and _ _ _ _ _ _ _ are what some children are grateful for.

5. Being grateful for _ _ _ _ _ _ _ people and events is important.

DOWN:

1. Being grateful means _ _ _ _ _ _ _ _ _ _ _ _ your abilities.

2. Being grateful means _ _ _ _ _ _ _ _ your family you appreciate them.

3. You show gratitude when you feel _ _ _ _ _ _ _ _ _ to have something.

4. Being _ _ _ _ _ _ _ _ _ _ is when you are envious of the talents of others.

5. Being _ _ _ _ _ _ _ _ for your friends show gratitude.

SELECT YOUR ANSWERS FROM THE FOLLOWING WORDS.
ANSWERS CAN BE FOUND ON PAGE 232.

thankful	important	grateful	telling	ungrateful
fortunate	special	appreciating	friends	grateful

Secret Code

Name: _____ Class: _____ Date: _____

DECODE THE WORD IN EACH SENTENCE.

1. Being grateful for _ _ _ _ _ _ _ people
   and events is important.   zieulcn

2. Being grateful means _ _ _ _ _ _ _ _ your
   family you appreciate them.   tennlhj

3. Being _ _ _ _ _ _ _ _ _ _ is when you
   are envious of the talents of others   ahjfctesan

4. You should be _ _ _ _ _ _ _ _ for people
   who take care of you.   jfctesan

5. It is _ _ _ _ _ _ _ _ _ not to take
   people for granted.   lpidftcht

6. You show gratitude when you feel
   _ _ _ _ _ _ _ _ _ to have something.   sdftahcte

7. Being _ _ _ _ _ _ _ _ _ for your friends
   shows gratitude.   tochvsan

8. Parents, food, clothes, toys and _ _ _ _ _ _ _
   are what some children are grateful for.   sflehkz

9. Gratitude is being _ _ _ _ _ _ _ _ for things
   others do for you.   jfctesan

10. Being grateful means _ _ _ _ _ _ _ _ _ _ _ _ your abilities.   ciifeulctlhj

Secret Code:

a b c d e f g h i j k l m n o p q r s t u v w x y z
u b a o e r v n p g d i x l h m q z f t c k w j y s

SELECT YOUR ANSWERS FROM THE FOLLOWING WORDS.
ANSWERS CAN BE FOUND ON PAGE 232.

| telling | important | ungrateful | fortunate | friends |
| special | appreciating | grateful | thankful | grateful |

Word Search

Name: _____ Class: _____ Date: _____

TRY TO FIND THE HIDDEN WORDS.

```
H Q E W K V O I M P O R T A N T G E
V R T A E O O W F R I E N D S F S O
V Q C P Q O U N G R A T E F U L P D
T X R P W C A J E G D G X N H N P V
R R X R G R A T E F U L B Y V X Y R
V T H E D T W K G N O T R I T U D Q
F X L C S Q V A Y P O H C N E J A S
D O E I C F H G C G N A B H M S C W
R D R A G X S T S D D N Q I N H I U
V D H T A N U K I A N L K L U U I P
D V B I U Z W S G T E F B S J L X O
M N G N B N W T R B E U U P H P P G
U X P G H T A S A Y M L U E E L Q S
K N E R P Z I T T Z J I L C H I M L
N H E O M Q X S E Z Z B L I E S K D
K H R G Y Y P N F D L T F A N H G N
J D Q E B O H Z U H U X M L X G M O
Z Z I K I R D V L F L V R F W V J R
```

SELECT FROM THE FOLLOWING WORDS.
ANSWERS CAN BE FOUND ON PAGE 232.

appreciating	thankful	special	telling	grateful
important	grateful	friends	fortunate	ungrateful

Answers

Secret Code page 230

1. special
2. telling
3. ungrateful
4. grateful
5. important
6. fortunate
7. thankful
8. friends
9. grateful
10. appreciating

Crossword Puzzle page 229

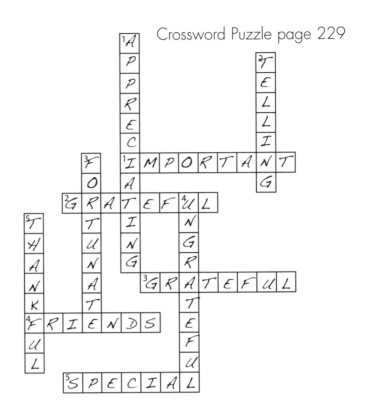

Word Search page 231

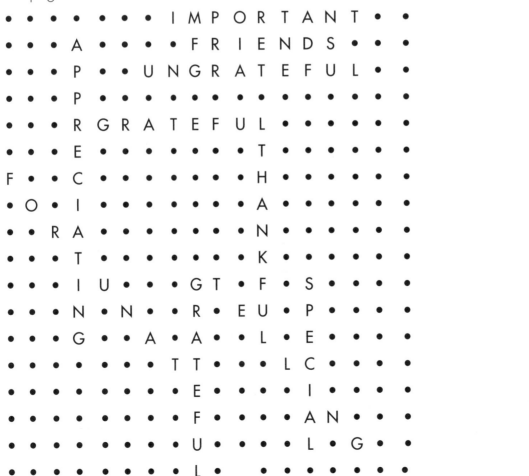

Chapter Thirteen

Graduation
Transition

Students make many transitions during their years of schooling: from home to school, elementary to middle school, middle school to high school and high school to work or college. These transitions are usually major events in the lives of students and parents. The stresses created by these transitions can be reduced if the new environment is made to be familiar and the old environment is supportive. New environments can be explored with school tours and open house nights for families. Here are some suggestions to ease the life transition of leaving elementary school.

Letters

All sorts of letters can be written to help students process the transition and give closure to the process. Here are some suggestions:

1. Have the students write a letter to next year's incoming class giving them advice on what they wished they would have known at the beginning of last school year. You would collect these letters, preview them and distribute to next year's class. Each year continues the tradition.

2. Have students write their next year's teacher a letter telling the teacher a little about themselves and what their worries are as well as to what they are looking forward to.

3. Have students take this opportunity to write a teacher who has made a difference in their lives a thank you letter. A story to illustrate this point for the students would be if you read them *Thank you, Mr. Falker* by Patricia Polacco. Then you distribute the letters after previewing them.

4. Have your students write a letter to themselves reviewing and processing the past school year. A template for this letter is in the lesson.

Using the school's video camera, make a tape to share with the students. Here are some ideas for the tape.

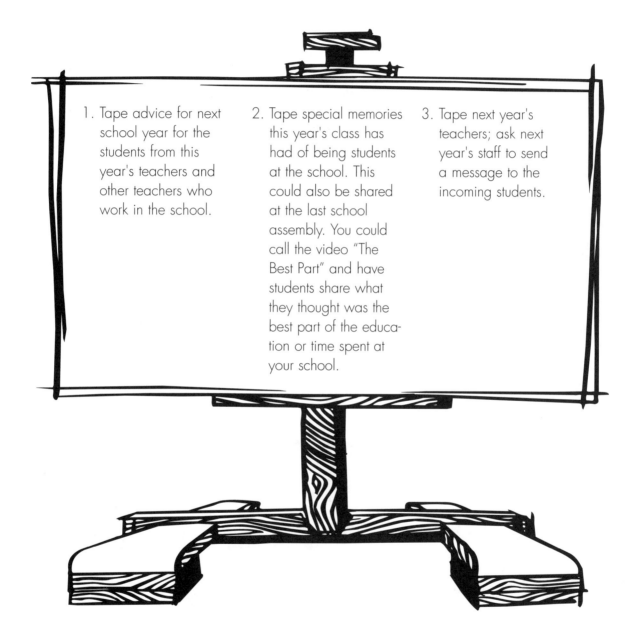

1. Tape advice for next school year for the students from this year's teachers and other teachers who work in the school.

2. Tape special memories this year's class has had of being students at the school. This could also be shared at the last school assembly. You could call the video "The Best Part" and have students share what they thought was the best part of the education or time spent at your school.

3. Tape next year's teachers; ask next year's staff to send a message to the incoming students.

Quotation Cards

Using card stock, run off business-size cards that may be cut and laminated to give to your students to keep in their wallets, purses or backpacks to remember your character lessons. Perhaps parent volunteers could assist on this large task. Here are some quotes to consider:

"The measure of a person's character is what he would do if he were never found out."

Thomas Macaulay

"To do good things in the world, first you must know who you are and what gives meaning in your life."

Paula P. Brownlee

"I do the very best I know how—the very best I can and I mean to keep doing so until the end."

Abraham Lincoln

"Respect yourself if you would have others respect you."

Baltasar Gracian

TRANSITION

Children love to play games; create a year in review game based on a television game like:

- WHO WANTS TO BE A MILLIONAIRE
Generate a list of questions that reflect important points in the school year's lessons. Select a game contestant and other players based on the game show format.

- JEOPARDY
Create game categories and have five cards under each category. The categories and cards reflect important points in the school year's lessons. Each question gets harder as the number of points gets higher under each category.

- BINGO
Give students a blank Bingo Card and write the words for them to select from to complete their card. The words on the board reflect important points in the school year's lessons. You can review each point as you call out that concept.

- PASSWORD
Divide the class into two teams. One member of each team comes to the front of the class in front of the blackboard. Above their heads write a single word that reflects an important lesson point from the past year. The students standing in front of the class take turns calling on their teammates for one-word clues. After each clue is given the person in front gets a chance to guess. The team earns points when the word is guessed or if the other team has a member who accidentally says the word.

Graduation / Books

TRANSITION

OBJECTIVE:
- At the end of the lesson the students will be able to recall the lessons they have learned at their school.

- At the end of the lesson the students will be able to explain that although they are moving from their old school to a new one they are taking with them valuable life lessons.

MATERIALS:
needed for the lesson: box, backpack or suitcase, labels attached to common school items in a bag and a story or poem "Remember" to end the lesson.

OPTIONAL MATERIALS:
Mover's hat or T-Shirt. You could enter with it on and say, "I'm from _____ Moving to get you packed to move to _____(name of school)."

"SHOOTING STAR APPLAUSE":
Clap hands once, when clap hands again and with right hand have your star shoot off to the right. Why shooting star applause? Because we are going to shoot for the stars and be our very best at our new school!

1. Introduce the lesson by telling the students you are here to pack them up to move to their new school, and that it is time to say goodbye and pack.

   OPTIONAL: Mover's T-Shirt or Hat could be used to get their attention.

2. You will be reviewing the character lessons you have taught throughout the school year as well as what other grade level teachers have taught the students. You will be packing these items in a suitcase, backpack or box. Bring the items in a bag so students cannot see what you have in it.

3. Discuss each item as you pack it into the container. What did we learn about this? Or remind them what they learned. After you are done packing, read the story or poem. If you choose any of the stories listed, let them lend themselves to discussion about life and adapting to change. So have a follow up discussion based on the story.

4. End the lesson by reminding the class that they will never forget their old school because of the wonderful memories and lessons they have learned here. Or end the lesson by sharing the poem.

Books TRANSITION
Oh, the Places You' ll Go—Dr. Seuss
I Knew You Could—Craig Dorfman
Under the Big Sky—Treavor Romain
The North Star—Peter H. Reynolds

Lesson Preparation

You will be preparing the objects that will be used in the lesson to help the students process and remember the education they received at your school.

MATERIALS NEEDED:

labels that you have printed on your computer and laminated, common school items, masking tape to attach labels and bag.

PREPARATION NEEDED:

- Have a label made that you can attach to the suitcase, backpack or box that says: "Items to move with Mr./Mrs____ (teacher's name) Class to _____ (student's name)"

- Suggestions for labels:

  Caring

  Fairness

  Responsibility

  Perseverance

  Sportsmanship

  Leadership

  Confidence

  Gratitude

  Determination

  Friendship

  Respect

  Kindness

  Trustworthiness

  Generosity

  Goodwill

  Forgiveness

  Honesty

  Courage

  Memories

  Life Lessons

  Good Education

  Appreciation for: Art, Music, Sports, Library, Computers and Counseling

Remember BY MARTY SHARTS

Remember that the best way to reach the stars is to have a plan to get there.
Plans require work, so work hard.

Remember you really do know quite a lot.
But you will never know all that you need to know so never stop learning.

Remember that wanting to learn about new things is natural
but trying and experimenting with all of them is not.

Remember if you were tempted to make a bad choice, ask yourself this simple
question,"Would I do this if my mother were here?" It works every time.

Remember that it your right to take advantage of what life has to offer you.
But it is your responsibility to give more than you take.

Remember to stand up for what you believe in, even if you are the only one standing.
Your opinion matters.

Remember it is great to be right, but reminding others you are is not.

Remember if you scratch any one of us just below the surface, we are all the same.

Remember differences in people are good but pointing them out is not.

Remember mistakes are only bad mistakes if you keep repeating them.

Remember that without sad times, you don't really appreciate the happy times.

And finally, remember to make this world a better place one day at a time.

Dear Me, Myself and I

DEAR ME, MYSELF AND I,

Today I seem to be thinking a lot about the future and the past. It seems like a good time to reflect on what I have learned in my time at this school and to make some plans for what I want to accomplish next year. As I look back over my time at this school, it seems like a pretty good experience. I learned more about _____ than I ever thought I would. I understand these things better than I did last year:

— _____

— _____

Something I accomplished while at this school that I feel proud about is _____

_____.

My favorite teacher at this school is _____ because_____.

A good memory of this school that I will take with me is _____

_____.

I believe I will do well next year because _____

_____.

Here are three goals I have for myself next year:

Friend Goal—_____

Family Goal—_____

School Goal—_____

In closing, I want to remind myself that I had some very good experiences happen to me at this school, and there are many people here who care about me. I am special, and I will treat myself with respect and caring. I will show responsibility in all that I do and if I want good things to happen to me next year, I have the potential within myself to make this happen.

My special person,

Bulletin Board Ideas

Create interactive bulletin boards or walls in the school. Let the students add their memories to the board.

1. "THE THING I WILL REMEMBER MOST"
   You start the project by adding a positive message to the class that is leaving. Have cut pieces of paper for them to pick up and return to the memory mailbox that you have created. Then you post their memories on the board.

2. "THE BEST ADVICE"
   Have the faculty give words of wisdom and advice to this year's class which is leaving. Run off a template that says:

   The best life lesson I ever learned was:

   _____

   _____

   _____

   Teacher's Name

   Have the teachers return them to you and post their advice.

3. " HOW TO SUCCEED IN SCHOOL!"
   Have this year's class which is leaving write advice or words of wisdom to the students who remain. Use the same design as above only substitute the Student's Name where Teacher's Name is.

SCHOOL TRANSITION

Students make many transitions during their years of schooling: from home to school, elementary to middle school, middle school to high school and high school to work or college. These transitions are usually major events in the lives of students and parents. The stresses created by these transitions can be reduced if the new environment is made to be familiar and the old environment is supportive. Here are some suggestions to ease the life transition of leaving elementary school.

* Take a tour of the new school. Bring questions you have to ask your new principal and teachers.

* Have your student get organized. It will be easier if you have a system for your belongings and your schoolwork.

* Encourage your student to join clubs, and participate in sports and as many activities as he can. These will help him meet people and he will feel he is a part of his new school.

* If your student needs advice, assistance or general moral support during his first few weeks, make sure he knows who to ask. School counselors, principals and office staff are trained and used to easing the transition.

As their parent, remember the goal of parenting is independence, the ability for your children to be able to make good decisions and learn to take care of themselves. Parenting is about roots and wings. Roots so your child will know the values, ideals and life lessons your family has taught her to give her a firm foundation. And wings so that she may soar to reach her dreams, goals and grow to be the person she is to be.

References

INTRODUCTION

Elbot, C. (2000). *Shaping the future through character education.* Denver, Co: Colorado State Conference on Character Education. (ERIC Document Reproduction Service No. ED 468 627)

CHAPTER 1

Sedita, J. (1995). *A call for more study skills instruction.* Orlando, FL: International Conference of the Learning Disabilities Association. (ERIC Document Reproduction Service No. ED 380 973)

Thomas, A. (1993). *Study skills.* (Report No. ISSN-0095-6694) Eugene, OR: Oregon School Study Council. (ERIC Document Reproduction Service No. ED 355 616)

Wheeler, P. (1993). *Preparing students for testing: should we promote test wiseness? EREAPA publication series No. 93-1.* Livermore, CA (ERIC Document Reproduction Service No. ED 374 163)

CHAPTER 2

American Academy of Child & Adolescent Psychiatry. (1998, November). *Children and grief.* Retrieved February 18, 2006, from http://www.aacap.org/publications/factsfam/grief.htm

Hopsice of Cincinnati. (n.d.). *Handling grief at school* [Brochure]. Cincinnati, OH: Author.

Slater, E. (1992). *Relationships and family living.* St. Paul, MN: EMC Publishing.

CHAPTER 3

About National Grandparents Day. (n.d.). Retrieved January 30, 2006, from http://www.grandparents-day.com/shortver.htm

North Dakota State University Extension Service. (1994, April). *The influence of grandparents and stepgrandparents on grandchildren.* Retrieved February 4, 2006 from http://www.ext.nodak.edu/extpubs/y/famsci/fs548w.htm

CHAPTER 4

Halloween. (2006). *Encyclopedia Britannica.* Retrieved March 19, 2006 from Encyclopedia Britannica Premium Service. http:www.britannica.com/eb/article-9038951

The History Channel. (n.d.) *The history of halloween.* Retrieved January 20, 2006 from http//www.historychannel.com/exhibits/Halloween/?page=origins

National Center for Missing and Exploited Children. (n.d.) *Halloween safety tips.* Retrieved February 13, 2006 from http://www.missingkids.com

The National Crime Prevention Council.
(n.d.) *Home and neighborhood safety.*
Retrieved February 13, 2006 from
http://www.mcgruff.org

Pumpkins. (2006). *Encyclopedia Britannica.*
Retrieved March 19, 2006 from
Encyclopedia Britannica Premium Service.
http:www.britannica.com/eb/article-
9061895

CHAPTER 5

The National Center on Addiction and
Substance Abuse at Columbia University.
(2003, September.). Retrieved March 20,
2006, from http://www.casafamily-
day.org

North Carolina Cooperative Extension
Service.(n.d.).*Family traditions strengthen
families.* Retrieved March 15, 2006,
from http://www.ces.ncsu.edu/success-
fulfamily/Human%20Development/-
famtrad.htm

CHAPTER 6

Cheyenne. (2006). *Encyclopedia Britannica.*
Retrieved May 23, 2006, From Encyclopedia
Britannica Premium Service
http://www.britannica.com/eb/article-
9023921

Cohlene, Terri. (1990). *Quillworker a
Cheyenne legend.* Vero Beach, FL.:
Rourke.

Dominic, Gloria. (1990). *Clamshell boy a
Makah legend.* Vero Beach, FL.: Rourke.

Dominic, Gloria. (1996). *Coyote and the
grasshoppers a Pomo legend.* Vero
Beach, FL.: Rourke.

Dominic, Gloria. (1996). *Red Hawk and
the Sky Sisters a Shawnee legend.* Vero
Beach, FL.: Rourke.

Dominic, Gloria. (1996). *Sunflower's
promise a Zuni legend.* Vero Beach, FL.:
Rourke.

Ilhawaii. (n.d.). *Quotes from our native past.*
Retrieved May 23, 2006, from
http://www.ilhawaii.net/~stony/-
quotes.html

Navajo. (2006). *Encyclopedia Britannica.*
Retrieved May 23, 2006.from
Encyclopedia Britannica Premium Service
http://www.britannica.com/eb/article-
9055069

Nootka. (2006). *Encyclopedia Britannica.*
Retrieved May 23, 2006. from
Encyclopedia Britannica Premium Service
http://www.britannica.com/eb/article-
9056086

Shawnee. (2006). *Encyclopedia Britannica.*
Retrieved May 23, 2006. from
Encyclopedia Britannica Premium Service
http://www.britannica.com/eb/article-
9067193

Zuni. (2006). *Encyclopedia Britannica*. Retrieved May 23, 2006. from Encyclopedia Britannica Premium Service http://www.britannica.com/eb/article-9078494

CHAPTER 7

National Collegiate Athletic Association. (2006). *Encyclopedia Britannica*. Retrieved January 19, 2006, from Encyclopedia Britannica Premium Service http:www.britannica.com/eb/article-9054968

Olympics. (2006). *Encyclopedia Britannica*. Retrieved January 19, 2006, from Encyclopedia Britannica Premium Service http:www.britannica.com/eb/article-9125322

Super Bowl. (2006). *Encyclopedia Britannica*. Retrieved January 19, 2006, from Encyclopedia Britannica Premium Service http:www.britannica.com/eb/-article-9070385

World Series. (2006). *Encyclopedia Britannica*. Retrieved May 21, 2006, from Encyclopedia Britannica Premium Service http://www.britannica.com/-eb/article-9077495

Youth Sports. (n.d.). *Teaching youngsters how to be good sports*. Retrieved April 17, 2006, from http://youth-sports.com

CHAPTER 8

The History Channel. (n.d.) *Black history month*. Retrieved February 6, 2006, from http://www.historychannel.com

Tobin, J. & Dobard, R. (1999). *Hidden in plain view*. New York: Random House.

"Tubman, Harriet." (2006). *Encyclopedia Britannica*. Retrieved January 20, 2006 , from Encyclopedia Britannica Premium Service. http:www.britannica.com/eb/article-9073673

Underground Railroad. (2006). *Encyclopedia Britannica*. Retrieved January 29, 2006, from Encyclopedia Britannica Premium Service http:www.britannica.com/eb/article-9074229

Vaughan, M. (2001, May). *The secret to freedom*. New York: Lee and Low.

Waber, B. (2002), *Courage*. New York: Houghton Mifflen.

CHAPTER 9

Groundhog Day. (2006). *Encyclopedia Britannica*. Retrieved May 21, 2006, from Encyclopedia Britannica Premium Service http://www.britannica.com/eb/article-9038219

Superstitions. (n.d.). *Old superstitions*. Retrieved May 21, 2006, from http://www.oldsuperstitions.com

World Book. (1992). *All about holidays* (pp. 8-9), Chicago, IL. World Book.

CHAPTER 10

The History Channel. (n.d.) *The history of valentine's day.* Retrieved February 6, 2006 from http://www.historychannel.com

Valentine's Day. (2006). *Encyclopedia Britannica.* Retrieved February 17, 2006, from Encyclopedia Britannica Premium Service. http:www.britannica.com/eb/-article-9074694

CHAPTER 11

April Fools' Day. (2006). *Encyclopedia Britannica.* Retrieved May 21, 2006, from Encyclopedia Britannica Premium Service http://www.britannica.com/-eb/article-9008096

Kids Health. (2006, January). *Encouraging your child's sense of humor.* Retrieved May 21, 2006, from http://www.kid-shealth.org/parent/growth/learning/-child humor.html

Motivational Quotes. (n.d.). *Motivational humor quotes.* Retrieved May 21, 2006, from http://www.quotationsbaout.com/-cs/inspirationquotes/a/Funny13.html

CHAPTER 12

Father's Day. (2006). *Encyclopedia Britannica.* Retrieved May 17, 2006, from Encyclopedia Britannica Premium Service http://www.britannica.com/-eb/article-9389225

Mother's Day. (2006). *Encyclopedia Britannica.* Retrieved May 17, 2006, from Encyclopedia Britannica Premium Service http://www.britannica.com/-eb/article-9389227

World Book. (1992). *All about holidays* (pp.16-17), Chicago, IL. World Book.

CHAPTER 13

Motivational Quotes. (n.d.). *Motivational character quotes.* Retrieved May 21, 2006, from http://www.quotations-baout.com/cs/inspirationquotes/a/-Funny13.html

About the Author

Martha A. Sharts is a veteran teacher and school counselor with a graduate degree from the University of Dayton in Dayton, Ohio. She received her bachelor's degree from The Ohio State University, in Columbus, Ohio. She is a member of the Ohio School Counselor Association and the American School Counseling Association.

She currently works as an elementary counselor with Miamisburg City Schools in Miamisburg, Ohio. Her experience includes conducting diversity training for high school and university audiences. Her classes have been featured on local television programs examples of excellence in education.

She has been recognized for her contributions to the field of education through numerous achievements and awards. She has been named Exemplary Teacher by the Miamisburg City Schools and recognized by them for her "best practice" in outstanding educational lessons. She has received The Outstanding Achievement Award for School Conflict Management from the Ohio Commission on Dispute Resolution and Conflict Management. She has presented for the Ohio School Board Association, the National Conference for Conflict Resolution and at various state counseling association conventions.